media

MANUAL

audio for single camera operation

media

MANUAL

media

MANUAL

audio for single camera operation

tony grant

Focal Press

OXFORD AMSTERDAM BOSTON LONDON NEW YORK PARIS
SAN DIEGO SAN FRANCISCO SINGAPORE SYDNEY TOKYO

Focal Press
An imprint of Elsevier Science
Linacre House, Jordan Hill, Oxford OX2 8DP
200 Wheeler Road, Burlington MA 01803

First published 2003

British Library Cataloguing in Publication Data
Grant, Tony
  Audio for single camera operation. – (Media manual)
  1. Sound – Recording and reproducing   2. Video recording
  I. Title
  778.5'92

Library of Congress Cataloguing in Publication Data
A catalogue record for this book is available from the Library of Congress

ISBN 0 240 51644 3

For information on all Focal Press publications visit our website at:
www.focalpress.com

Typeset by Keyword Typesetting Services Ltd
Printed and bound in Great Britain by Biddles Ltd, *www.biddles.co.uk*

Contents

About the author

Tony Grant began his career in broadcasting with the BBC, and first worked in the sound department at Television Centre, but later transferred to the camera department. He has worked in studios, on OBs, and on single camera locations at home and abroad, both as a cameraman and latterly as DoP. Throughout his career he has been actively involved with training, both in craft and production skills. Over the past few years he has organized and lectured on many training courses for several organizations including the BBC, ITV companies, cable and satellite, Ravensbourne College, the GTC and the BKSTS. He has written a wide variety of technical articles for the trade press, and has been freelance for the past few years.

Acknowledgements

I should like to express my thanks to the many sound recordists, mixers, supervisors and dubbing editors I've worked with over the years, would that I had room to list you all. However, I must give a special mention to my friends Colin Berwick, Colin Bowman and Peter Brand, who devoted much time and effort in patiently answering all my queries, as well as reading incomplete manuscripts. Other friends and colleagues who have, perhaps unwittingly, contributed to the information and techniques described herein, but with whom I've enjoyed the pleasure of working over the past few years, include Gavin Bateman, Dave Batt, Barry Cobden, Peter Coles, Tom Gilmore, Tony Glossop, Rob Kreeger, Rob Miles and Brian Roberts.

Regarding illustrative material contained within the book, I would like to thank Bill Curtis at Ravensbourne College for his assistance with much of the photography, together with all my 'models' – I'm sorry I'm unable to thank you all individually. I am also indebted to Ambient Recording GmbH for permission to reproduce the illustration of the Lockit Box and to the publishers for permission to reproduce several illustrations from both *The Microphone Book* and *Multiskilling for Television Production*.

Should you encounter any errors or mistakes from here on, they have nothing to do with any of the aforementioned and are completely my own.

Tony Grant

Introduction

'Every picture tells a story', so we've always been told, and pictures frequently dominate the thinking within our industry. But although a television set seems to 'pull' your eyes towards it when it's on, how long would it hold your attention without any sound? No, I'm not going to debate whether sound or pictures are more important ... that depends on subject and context. But what I will assert is that both must be 'telling the same story'. If the pictures and sound appear unrelated at any point, the viewer will be distracted. He or she may not realize why they're having difficulty following a programme, but subliminally they will be disturbed, and may well change channels or switch off. Not the effect we're striving to achieve! Not only should the sound match and enhance the pictures, the viewer should remain unaware of the technical considerations involved. The exercise of any craft skill should be transparent to the audience.

Thus, the emphasis herein is on listening to sound via a microphone, and ensuring that the signal it produces, and that you record, provides the viewer/listener with the sound that he/she expects to accompany the pictures they are watching. Our ear/brain combination is extremely sophisticated in processing the sounds we hear, interpreting distance, direction, frequency, loudness and other qualities. The mic and the sound system are not! They simply pass electrical information through a series of circuits until it's reproduced by a loudspeaker, leaving the listener's ear/brain to interpret the result. So as a recordist, you have to ensure that the resultant sound is realistic, or perhaps a better word is 'believable', as an accompaniment to the pictures.

I make no apology for the fact that the one item I repeat at regular intervals throughout is that you *must* know how your recorded material is to be used, in other words, you need an understanding of the post-production process. Most of the material you record is likely to undergo some form of post production before it's heard by your intended audience. Therefore, you must be certain that you're able to provide the 'type' of sound needed to provide sufficient flexibility for the dubbing editor to modify *if necessary* in order to match the pictures, which may themselves be altered or 'treated' during the post-production process. Throughout the audio chain, both at acquisition and the subsequent dubbing and editing, all involved must be aware of how the sound will be reproduced for listeners, together with their probable listening environment. The digital recording quality now available has improved the dynamic range available to the recordist, but the television transmission system is unable to cope with too wide a dynamic range. Most domestic environments, for instance, have a relatively high background noise level, thus rendering any very low sound levels in your recorded material ineffectual.

For those of you at the start of your career, I hope that within this handbook you can find all you need to begin to tread the path of the Sound Recordist alongside a single video camera on location. Working 'hand in glove' with a cameraman and acquiring high quality sound may seem a daunting prospect, but like driving a car, it's all down to 'hands-on' experience. From that point of view, I would suggest you endeavour to work as an assistant alongside an experienced recordist before taking the plunge yourself.

At the same time, single person operation has also become a regular method of working in many areas of broadcasting, and so several sections of the book address the limitations this places on sound acquisition alongside other operational responsibilities. Another facet of broadcasting is multi-skilling, and some operators may only spend part of their time working as a sound recordist. To this end, I have included a broad overview of planning location work from a recce through to assembling equipment and understanding a call sheet, together with checklists of do's and don'ts regarding safe operational practice and the rigging and de-rigging of equipment.

Although the industry is moving away from the use of Beta SP as the *de facto* recording standard towards digital formats, I have made reference to it in some sections of the book. This is because it has been in use on location for over ten years, and will continue to be found in many parts of the world for up to another ten. The difference in acquisition techniques, however, should not be affected by the choice of recording format.

Unfortunately, the book's structure cannot take into account every reader's present knowledge, experience and aspirations, although I have attempted to present the information in a logical manner. Having read it through, therefore, you may find that you subsequently have to skip backwards and forwards in order to correlate the sections and topics to your particular skill level and method/s of operation.

As your career progresses, you will find that not only do operational methods and production styles change over time, so too does technological advancement *vis-à-vis* equipment design, frequently necessitating a re-appraisal of the skills and techniques necessary for sound acquisition. Therefore, treat the contents of this book and the techniques outlined within as a starting point. As your experience grows, together with the type and amount of equipment you carry, you will often need to modify aspects of your operation in order to adapt to changing practices within the industry.

Before we start

This book grew out of articles written for *Zerb*, the journal for the Guild of Television Cameramen, and at the beginning of these I asserted that you only need two things to record good sound, and they were to be found on either side of your head – yes, your ears! The point I was making was that *listening* is all important. So, before you set foot on location, you can begin to familiarize yourself with the basics of sound recording through listening to the end product, as well as working through the suggested practical recording exercises contained within the text.

Listen to as much broadcast and recorded sound as possible and judge the quality and clarity of what you hear, as well as any changes in volume or level relationships between differing sound sources. I would suggest that the best way to go about this is to listen to a variety of material on headphones, in order to gain future practical recording experience. If you can record some television programmes, play them first with your eyes closed, listening closely to the results, and make sure you can distinguish each aural element contained within the mix. Then replay the tape with your eyes open, and notice what a difference the pictures make to both understanding and interpreting the sound. Take, for example, a vocalist singing to a musical accompaniment; can you distinguish each individual instrument, as well as understand the words being sung? Proceeding in this way, you can begin to discern the difference between good and bad sound balance and relative levels.

Adjust your own listening level, via the volume control, and notice how, as you turn it up, the low and high frequencies appear to increase relative to the overall signal. The ear's sensitivity to frequency changes with volume, and thus altering the volume will affect the perceived tonal quality. Therefore, when you are recording, you must always ensure that you monitor your sound at a constant – and comfortable(!) – listening level. Take care – do not listen to high levels of sound for any length of time, you could permanently damage your hearing by doing so.

1 I'm all ears – theoretically!

There are many aspects to sound and hearing that most of us take for granted. Our ear/brain combination is capable of extremely sophisticated discrimination, enabling us to concentrate selectively on sound from one or two sources within a complex aural background; which may often comprise sound from many sources arriving at our ears simultaneously. Thus, before we start to use a mic, let's delve into some basic sound theory, so that we're aware of why things may not always turn out as expected.

Sound – the executive explanation

Whilst sitting at your desk, pick up an elastic band, and stretch it between the thumb and forefinger of one hand (Figure 1.1(a)–(c)). Whilst watching the band, pluck it with one finger from your other hand – twang – ah, you heard that! And I'm sure you also saw that its vibrations caused the noise.

Well, in a nutshell that's the nature of sound in air. As you 'pluck' the elastic band, it vibrates, and the energy thus released pushes the particles (molecules) of air forwards (compression) and backwards (rarefaction) in time with its vibrations. These waves travel through the air, the energy they contain is transmitted to your eardrum, and you hear the 'twang'.

(a)

Figure 1.1 Listen to the band

(b)

(c)

Fig. 1.1 continued

Furthermore, the closer you hold the band to your ear, the louder it sounds (see also Section 2, Sound measurement; Inverse Square Law), and the 'harder' you pluck the band, the louder the sound. The tauter you hold the band, the higher the note you hear, and if you watch closely, you'll see that it vibrates more quickly as it gets tauter. Thus, the *frequency* of the sound you hear is related to the number of compressions and rarefactions arriving at your eardrum within a fixed time (cycles per second, see also Section 2, Sound measurement; Frequency).

If you're a really top executive, you can carry this experiment to extreme lengths by filling one ear with cotton wool, closing your eyes, and getting your personal assistant to twang the elastic band at differing distances from your unblocked ear. You'll notice that you can easily tell when the twang is close to you, and when it is further away. However, if your assistant also varies the direction, say within a 180° arc, keeping to the 'unblocked' side of your head (so that you definitely can't hear it in your blocked ear) (Figure 1.2), then you'll find it impossible to perceive the direction from which the sound is coming. And that's what you'd expect to find (hear) if you were using a mono microphone in place of your ear!

Home-loving executives, before you bath the kids, once you've filled the bath, pop their plastic duck in the middle, and send a wave rippling out from the side. The duck bobs *up and down* as the wave passes, but doesn't move *along* with it.

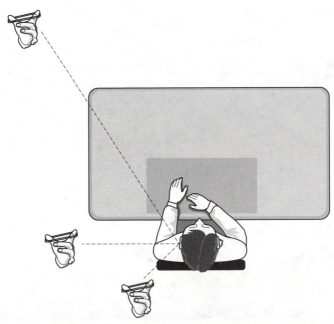

Figure 1.2 As your assistant moves around, you will be unable to determine from which direction the 'twang' comes, but you can tell how loud it is, and thus how close it is to you

(You may need to pop next door and borrow the neighbours' if you haven't got your own kids/bath/duck, etc.) The sound wave in air is similar in so far as individual molecules are compressed and rarefied, but stay within the same volume of space, whilst the wave spreads outward from the sound source.

I hear you knocking

Sound travels faster within solid materials than in air (gaseous transmission) and its transmission through them is often more efficient than through air. If you're in a building when someone starts some serious construction activity – hammering, drilling, etc. – you'll find the sound travels easily throughout the building, penetrating every nook and cranny, and the sound no longer appears to come from a point source. This can make it difficult to locate the source, but rendering any serious sound recording out of the question until you do so.

As an aside, I once undertook a recce on a Friday for a musical item to be recorded in the hall of a municipal building on the following day. It was extremely busy with many staff going backwards and forwards to their offices in the building, as well as members of the public making enquiries, etc. Nevertheless, we were assured that we'd have the hall to ourselves the following day. I even asked if they were expecting public access at any time during the day, but we were assured that the building was officially closed. Imagine our horror on arrival the following morning to find a team of decorators hard at work in the offices adjoining the hall!

So, on location you must be careful to avoid picking up noise or vibration transmitted through the floor when using a stand mic. Wooden floors are a real menace, as the simple act of walking across the floor can easily be picked up by a stand mic anywhere within the room. If there is a danger of this happening, the stand needs to be 'acoustically isolated' from the floor to minimize the disturbance, using some form of absorbent material – thick foam/sponge rubber (Figure 1.3), for example – even though the stand base may have rubber feet. The same often applies to a table stand, as any material being knocked or banged on the table will be transmitted – extremely efficiently – to the mic.

Hearing test

Before proceeding further, and attempting to turn this theory into practice, I would advise you to consider having your own hearing tested. I say this because, when I joined the BBC many years ago, part of the first training course I embarked upon had a form of 'do-it-yourself testing' for frequency perception in the shape of a variable oscillator. Of course, it was actually intended for checking the frequency response of various items of sound circuitry and equipment, not for the amusement of the great unwashed trainees in our group!

But ever eager to find out what else we could do with the technical equipment at our disposal, we rigged it up to a loudspeaker and turned the dial backwards and forwards, listening to the tone rising and falling in pitch. Through participating in this exercise I discovered that my hearing tailed off around 17 kHz, and that everyone else in our group could hear way above that frequency (most people can hear up to at least 20 kHz). Unfortunately, the

Figure 1.3 Foam or rubber under a stand can provide greater acoustic isolation, but do ensure that the stand is *stable* in its position

loudspeaker was too small to accurately reproduce any bass tones below 40 or 50 Hz, and so we were unable to ascertain what the bottom end of our individual responses might have been.

More recently, my daughter started to complain about her own hearing, and that many of the sounds she heard were often causing her considerable pain. A test subsequently revealed that she had extremely sensitive hearing, and that not only could some levels of sound be painful to her but also that she could perceive frequencies up to 24 kHz (she was forever complaining about our whistling television!). To complete the family picture, I should add that my wife has the opposite problem, being extremely hard of hearing, and often experiences difficulty with the intelligibility of sound on both radio and television, especially if there is any other noise present in the vicinity.

The point of these observations is to indicate the possibility that you may have a deficiency in your own hearing of which you are totally unaware. And if you intend to embark on a career involving sound recording, you should certainly make yourself aware of any limitations in your hearing before you proceed further. Many people find that one of their ears is more sensitive than the other, and that neither ear has exactly the same frequency response. Of course, once you know about any such discrepancies, you can make allowances within your working environment. Looking to the future, I would also advise you to have your hearing checked on a regular basis, say every couple of years, especially if you are in any way 'outside the norm'.

As you are probably aware, human hearing deteriorates with age, and the longer you live, the more you're likely to lose both sensitivity and frequency response at the top of the range (not that that's a reason to stop breathing just yet, of course!).

In sickness and in health

In a similar vein, you must be careful if you're unfortunate enough to experience any illnesses which affect your hearing. The common cold is the most likely culprit for this unpleasant experience amongst the community in general, and it really is best to have time off work than jeopardize both a shoot and your hearing. Trying to persist with some type of restriction in your hearing may lead you into monitoring sound at too high a level, and thus worsen your condition, if not leading to a degree of permanent hearing loss.

Without wishing to appear alarmist, there are some exceptionally nasty diseases around the world which can affect your hearing, and I can only recommend you seek medical advice at the first sign of any irritation, inflammation or blockage should you notice or experience one of these afflictions. Better a reputation as a hypochondriac than subsequently being unable to pursue your chosen career path.

2 Sound measurement

Although you're familiar by now with elastic bands (and plastic ducks!), you may not be quite so familiar with the terminology and figures used when measuring sound. Be aware though, that, as mentioned at the end of the previous section, with regard to human hearing, all figures given are approximate, since the absolutes vary from person to person, and hearing normally deteriorates with age and with any continued exposure to high sound levels (see Section 16, Safety). The human ear is sensitive to changes in loudness (level) but is more sensitive to changes in level within a specific range of frequencies – those covered by the voice.

Frequency

Hertz – Hz, is the SI unit representing the frequency of sound in cycles per second. In the same way that 'normal' human vision is termed 20/20, I like to think of 'normal' human hearing as being approximately '20/20', but that's 20 Hz to 20 kHz. The approximate range of human speech is about 75 Hz to 4 kHz (but there are also harmonics above these frequencies, depending on voice timbre).

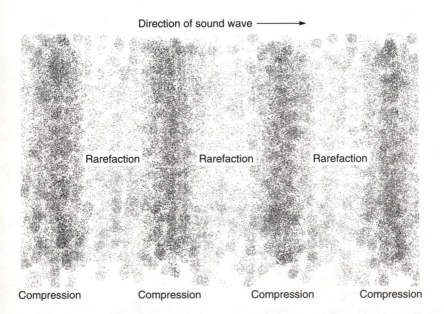

Figure 2.1 Compression and rarefaction of air molecules, sound travels at approximately 340 metres per second through the air

Velocity and wavelength

The higher the frequency, the shorter the wavelength of the sound. Without getting too technical, there's a mathematical relationship between frequency, wavelength and velocity:

$$\text{velocity} = \text{frequency} \times \text{wavelength}$$

Hey, that's not complicated, you say. Ah yes, but . . . the speed of sound in air – the main way we hear sound – depends on air temperature and pressure, and the presence of other particles in the air (humidity, pollution, etc.). It's usually quoted as being approximately 340 metres per second, and that's in still air. Additionally, you must expect air currents, wind, convection, etc. in normal surroundings, so you will appreciate how difficult it is to give meaningful figures for practical recording purposes – you can often hear sound 'carried on the wind' for considerable distances in the open air. The actual speed of sound in air doesn't alter, but the particles of air that transmit the sound energy are themselves moving, and essentially transporting the result over a greater distance in the direction the wind is blowing.

Doppler effect

However, if either the source, or the listener, begins to move, you become aware of the Doppler effect, a perceived alteration of the frequency. If the distance between source and listener is decreasing, the frequency is raised, and vice versa. Stand beside a busy road, with traffic moving at speed, and the effect is easily appreciated – 'Wheeeeoooow' – as we used to yell as kids. (See also Moving mics, below.)

Sound reflection and absorption

But in the normal course of events, you'd be forgiven for thinking that the speed of sound wouldn't unduly affect your work, especially using a mic relatively close to the sound source. However, although the *direct* sound may remain unaffected, *indirect*, or reflected sound, can easily add unwanted or unexpected colouration to the end result.

Depending on your environment, sound may be reflected or absorbed by the material covering objects/furniture/surfaces in your surroundings. And different wavelengths behave in different ways, for instance, wavelengths longer than the dimensions of an object tend to 'bend' around it, and may not be significantly impeded in their passage, whereas shorter wavelengths are more likely to be reflected and/or absorbed (see also Acoustics, below).

Thus it is perfectly possible for a sound from a particular source to appear clear or muddied or sharper or flatter than its 'true' or 'close-up' value as perceived by the ear (or mic) as you move around a location. This alteration in the precise nature of the perceived sound at a particular spot is what is meant when we use the term 'colouration', and care must be exercised in the placement of mics to avoid distorting effects produced in this way, especially if they sound unpleasant or unnatural (see also Moving Mics below).

Phase

Sound waves interact with each other when their wavelengths are the same, or as near as makes no difference, and this is mostly how colouration is produced. If the crests/peaks coincide, they add to each other, thus increasing their intensity (and, therefore, sounding louder) at that point in space, and they are said to be 'in phase'. If, on the other hand, they cancel each other out, you will be unable to hear any evidence of that frequency at that point, and they are said to be 'out of phase' (Figure 2.2(a),(b)). (A similar visible effect occurs when wave crests are reflected off a harbour wall, for example, and interact with oncoming waves, most noticeable where the cumulative effect is observed.)

Phase difference may be expressed in terms of degrees, thus 180° is out of phase (complete cancellation of waves), and 0° and 360° are in phase (cumulative waves). Phase differences outside these absolutes lend colouration to sound, either by adding to or subtracting from the intensity at a given frequency.

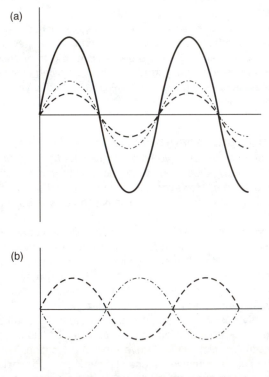

Figure 2.2 (a) Combining signals in graphical form from sound waves in phase increases intensity; (b) combining signals in graphical form from sound waves out of phase cancels the output

Phase difference is utilized in directional microphones, designed in such a way that sounds off axis tend towards cancellation. The success of any individual design is dependent on the physical size/length of the mic housing, and the size/distribution of 'ports' along its barrel (interference tube), limiting its range of frequency cancellation.

Moving mics

Phase problems are not necessarily limited to sound reflections, and can occur when using more than one mic. Should you move one of them relative to a fixed (static) sound source, or the source (e.g. person) moves relative to the mics, you will almost certainly find a phase difference between the sounds arriving at each mic. This is because a varying time differential has been introduced to the sound arriving at each mic, leading to some frequencies being enhanced and others attenuated (an effect known as comb filtering). The effect is at its most apparent, and unpleasant, when the speed of the mic, or source, keeps changing, continuously altering which frequencies are affected.

Thinking aloud

When measuring sound intensity we use a unit called the decibel, dB. It is a measurement of the relationship of one intensity to another, in other words, one sound is 'x' number of units (dBs) louder or quieter than another. It is based on a logarithmic scale, since this matches the way the ear responds to intensity.

But, in the world of sound, this unit has the potential for great misunderstanding. That is because it depends on which side of the mic capsule you take the measurement. On the real world, noisy side, you are measuring pressure differences/intensities, which activate the capsule, whilst on the signal side, you are measuring a varying voltage produced by the capsule. Would that the scientific fraternity had decided to appoint differing units to these measurements, but they opted for the dB in both cases.

Beware! Measurements relating to sound pressure/intensity produce an increase of 3 dB for a doubling in intensity; whereas with voltage (signal strength), a doubling produces an increase of 6 dB.

Since the measurements we use in recording, pertaining to our meters, are on the signal side of the mic, we are solely concerned with voltage variation, and so dB values quoted in the text assume that a rise of 6 dB indicates an increase in sound level by a factor of 2. This equates with the vision signal, where an increase of 6 dB indicates the equivalent to opening up one stop (a doubling of light level).

Inverse square law

Having mentioned a doubling of light, you're probably also aware of how its intensity falls off in relation to its distance from the source. The same law applies equally to sound. In still air, the energy of a sound wave is dissipated by the square of its distance from the original source (technically, this should be a 'point' source) (Figure 2.3). This means there are greater differences in level (dBs) close to a sound source of varying intensity than from a distance from that source. Thus, if a mic is positioned too close to someone's mouth, a clip mic on the neck of a T-shirt for example, the sound level is extremely sensitive to head movement. On the other hand, you can take advantage of the effect when operating a gun mic on a pole, by altering its distance from the speaker's mouth to accommodate the changes in voice level (Figure 2.4).

Acoustics

With an awareness and understanding of the technical considerations outlined above, we can apply this knowledge to the way we approach our operation in the 'real' world, and can begin to appreciate how we may best undertake our sound recording. For example, when we're working indoors, the dimensions of the location, and the fabrics on furniture and fittings, can influence the way sound is reflected (and absorbed), and this almost certainly 'colours' the overall

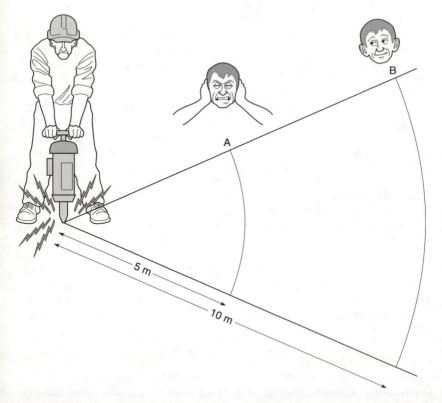

Figure 2.3 Inverse square law. The intensity of sound at point B is one quarter that of the intensity at point A

Figure 2.4   Vary the position of the mic to accommodate the changes in voice level

sound arriving at the mic. Hard surfaces reflect sound (the bathroom effect!) and large concert halls are usually designed to have a long sound decay (reverberation).

Therefore, if you're working in such a way that some colouration is unavoidable, as long as the camera is positioned to show the nature of the location, then the viewer accepts, for example, that a bathroom will echo more than a living room.

Intelligibility

However, to ensure the intelligibility of your sound, it's best to opt for a location that's as acoustically 'dead' as possible. Given the choice, pick a room with absorbent materials such as thick curtains and carpets and well-upholstered furniture. Avoid large flat surfaces, for example, bare walls, wood panelling, windows, glass-fronted cases, plain tables, etc. and don't work 'into' the corner of a room.

Carry some sound-deadening material/s with you, heavy drapes are useful, but may prove unwieldy for large areas. Caution: take care when gaffer taping or tying (or anything else!) to fixtures and fittings to stabilize them, they're unwieldy and have minds of their own. Wherever you are, always take care that you have enough room in which to work, especially if you're adding to surrounding clutter, and make sure you don't accidentally knock over valuable objets d'art! (see also Section 39, Insurance).

3 Camcorder: power and audio facilities

An *important* preliminary note:

The layout, labelling and position on the camcorder body of individual control panels, and the switches thereon, varies between each make and model, although each individual camcorder should have the functions described herein. Some of the functions, and the manner in which they operate, may also be altered through menu settings within the camcorder itself.

However, for the exact operational placement and switch labelling, and the parameters relating to menu functions, you must consult the relevant camcorder handbook.

Power

Most location operations rely on battery power for the camcorder. Broadcast models are normally run from 12 V rechargeable batteries, and have an operating range in the region of 10–14 V. The majority also have an external power supply connection in the form of a 4-pin XLR socket (Figure 3.1), and you can

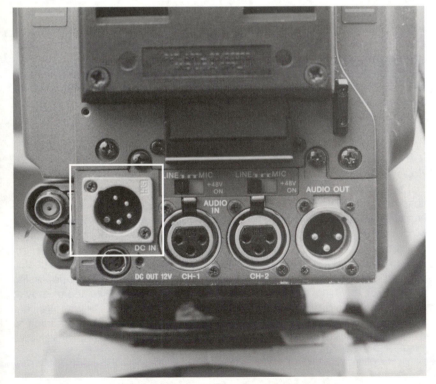

Figure 3.1   4-pin 12 V XLR power input on camcorder rear panel

Figure 3.2 LCD display on the side of the camcorder, showing the charge status of the battery

run them from a mains supply using a suitable transformer. The LCD display on the side of the camcorder often provides a rough indication of the voltage level, or the charge status of the battery (Figure 3.2). (See also Batteries and run time, below.)

On broadcast models, the power switch is usually located on the side body panel, and mounted in a horizontal operating position (Figure 3.3). One point to be aware of, on the front camera operational panel, there may be a switch position (often labelled 'VTR') for a *save* mode (Figure 3.4). In this condition, the camcorder is *on*, but the tape is not in contact with the record heads, in other words, this is a 'head saving' mode (this may instead be labelled camera/VTR in which case, the tape is not in contact with the heads in the camera position). It also has the unfortunate side-effect of not providing a sound feed to the camcorder monitoring facilities. Always make sure this is switched to the St/by (VTR) position which, although it will put the heads in contact with the tape, will provide you with your sound monitoring facilities. But if the cameraman is intent on minimizing the head wear, do remember to return it to the *save* position when you are satisfied with your levels.

Inputs

Most camcorders have XLR sockets for their sound inputs (Figure 3.5), although some of the smaller DV and mini DV models may have phono or 3.5 mm (mini) jack sockets (Figure 3.6). The advantage of the XLR connector is that it locks into position, and so cannot be pulled out accidentally, unlike the phono, with which this is a distinct possibility. Plus it is of a more robust and

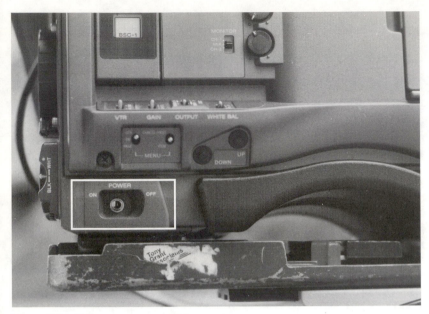

Figure 3.3 Camcorder power switch

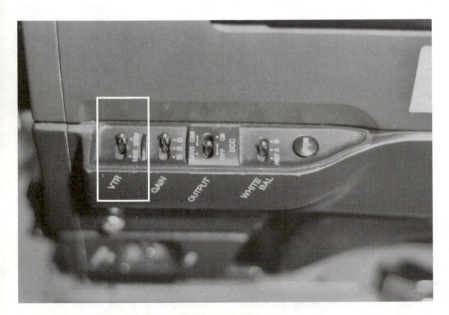

Figure 3.4 Camcorder VTR save/standby switch

Figure 3.5 Two 3-pin XLR inputs on camcorder rear panel

Figure 3.6 Mini DV camcorder with mini-jack socket mic input on front panel

rugged construction, thus less prone to mechanical damage and general wear and tear with everyday use.

Most camcorders have two sound inputs (normally referred to as 'channel' inputs), usually sited towards the bottom of the rear panel (Figure 3.7), and two soundtracks (upon which the audio is recorded). There are some models which provide four soundtracks, but accessing all four can often prove difficult and time-consuming, and not all edit suites are configured to accommodate them. Moreover, you may find that if you do use all four tracks, for example on DV systems, then the recorded sound will almost certainly be below broadcast standard in quality. Therefore, in this handbook we will only consider a camcorder to have two sound tracks available for recording purposes.

Sound output

Some camcorders provide outputs from either or both channels, which you may find useful for transcription recording (Figures 3.7 and 3.8). But if you do wish to use this for transcription purposes, note that most audio cassette recorders have mic level input, whilst the outputs on the camcorder are line level, i.e.

Figure 3.7 3-pin XLR inputs at rear of camcorder together with 3 pin XLR audio output beside them

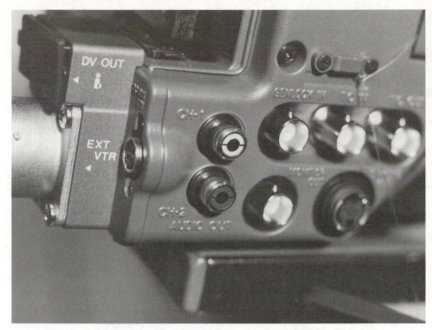

Figure 3.8 Sound output (on phono sockets)

amplified (see Section 4, Camcorder: track selection and magnetic recording). This means you will have to obtain/make up a connecting lead with a 60 dB pad (attenuation) to drop the level back down to mic voltage.

You may also find that some companies have modified their audio monitoring facilities to utilize the sound output from this socket/s, assuming that there is a signal present during the recording process. This will almost certainly mean that the headphones that you need to use in conjunction with this facility will have a more robust connector than the mini-jack, lending an increased reliability to this method of monitoring. However, in use, it does mean that the audio monitor level controls on the side of the camcorder do not affect this output, and that there must be some other form of level control available for your headphones (the modification to use this facility will probably take the form of a lead/s which plugs into the camcorder output socket/s and has a 'bodge-box' of some form with at least one, if not more, headphone sockets with volume control).

You should also be aware that using this facility in this way means that the feed to the on-board loudspeaker is not cut (since you have not plugged any headphones into the mini-jack monitoring socket on the side of the camcorder). Therefore you will almost certainly have to ensure that you turn these controls down to zero/off, in order to ensure that there is no breakthrough or disturbance from this source.

If you own your equipment and wish to utilize this method of audio monitoring, do make sure that the model of camcorder you have provides you with the sound output on the relevant socket/s during recording. (See also Section 7, Camcorder: external facilities – sound monitoring, for the mainstream information on monitoring the audio feed for normal recording purposes.)

Phantom power

On most camcorders this facility is switched above the XLR input socket (Figure 3.9), although on others it may be sited on the side panel of switches below the LCD display, or within the menu functions (see also Section 4, Camcorder: track selection and magnetic recording). Only turn it on if you are using a mic which needs this form of powering. Although the term 'phantom' implies that it shouldn't affect anything other than a mic which requires this facility, it is possible that a cable, wiring, connection, or other circuit fault could lead to a hum or buzz on the soundtrack if it's left on unnecessarily.

Batteries and run time

One of the most vexing questions you are likely to face is, 'How long does each battery last?' Judging by their external appearance, you have no way of telling,

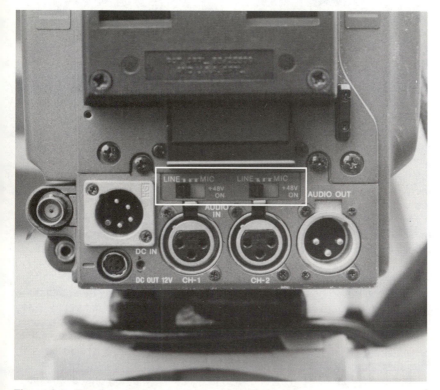

Figure 3.9 Phantom power switch (above each XLR input)

unless the battery has a readout of its charge status/voltage on its casing (I've only come across a couple of models that provide this facility). Once plugged/ connected to the camcorder, there may be a display on the LCD readout (Figure 3.2) showing the charge status, but this cannot be relied upon unless you have used that particular battery/camcorder combination before, and have confidence in the display's accuracy. When the batteries are new, and the camcorder has been correctly set internally (or via its menus) for the maximum battery voltage in use, then the display will almost certainly be accurate, but after the equipment has been in the field for any length of time, well, who knows?

Moreover, battery run time will be affected by the amount of power drain it's subjected to, and the functions it's required to operate. A quick run down of these will give you some idea of the rate at which you may deplete it's capacity, depending on how often you use:

■ picture processing and viewfinder
■ zoom
■ auto functions (iris, focus, etc.)
■ phantom power
■ run to record
■ cue (tally) lights on
■ LCD light on
■ on-camera lamp
■ power for external device from DC out on camcorder (e.g. radio mic receiver).

Hence there's no easy answer to the question of run time, and only experience with the individual items of equipment can be your judge. However, it is worth noting that having each individual battery labelled/numbered will save time if you suspect a fault. There is nothing more annoying than arriving back at base after a day's shoot, and not being able to recall which of half a dozen batteries had a problem, since they all look the same!

Warning! Should any battery have been dropped during the shoot, make sure that you put it to one side (and label or mark it accordingly as 'suspect') to be checked by a competent authority. Although it may still deliver power, and even appear to charge as per normal on its regular charger, it may actually be dangerous to use. Depending on the internal design/construction, individual cells within batteries are prone to fracture under external pressure, and in certain circumstances may overheat (and combust) if they, or their associated circuitry, have been damaged.

4 Camcorder: track selection and magnetic recording

Track selection

Once the audio feed/s have been plugged into the recorder, you must select the correct type for each track. Unfortunately, each model seems to have a layout and labelling system peculiar to itself, hence the need to refer to the appropriate manufacturer's handbook!

The camcorder record section may have a two-, three- or four-position switch, to select between on-camera mic, external/rear inputs, and possibly an onboard radio mic receiver or other facility specific to that model. You can, however, only switch the external input from channel one to track one of your recorder, and similarly the input from channel two to track two. In other words, via the camcorder switching you *cannot* select an input from one of the channels to both sound tracks on the recorder. The *only* facility that you can select to either (or both) tracks is the on-camera mic (see below) via the camcorder switching.

Mic and line level

There are usually two positions associated with 'rear', mic level and line level (Figure 4.1) for each track. The difference between mic and line level is normally in the region of 60 dB, that is mic level needs to be raised (amplified) 60 dB to bring it up to line level. This level of amplification is two to the power of ten, in other words the signal is amplified by a factor of (just over) a thousand.

If you're feeding a mic input, when you select 'mic' you may also need to select phantom power. Select line if you've plugged a separate source such as the feed from a PA desk, or a mixer. (A mic feed is relatively unamplified, whereas mixers and PA are amplified. If you incorrectly switch your rear inputs, you'll either be unable to hear anything – mic input selected at line level, or severe overload/distortion – 2^{10} – line level selected to mic level.)

On camera mic

This may be labelled 'front' or 'cam' on the selector switch (Figure 4.2). On broadcast models, it will almost certainly be automatically phantom powered when this position is selected. It may also be plugged via a short cable to an XLR socket on the camera body (Figure 4.3). This allows a degree of flexibility, for instance easy replacement of a faulty microphone (as it's a somewhat vulnerable position in which to site one), or the use of an alternative microphone in this position, or cabling another microphone directly to this socket (so long as you maintain the *camera* mic selected). But if you do plug another microphone to this socket (Figure 4.4) it will then automatically have phantom power along the cable.

Therefore, if you wish to use a dynamic mic in this configuration, check its output very carefully, as it might generate an unwanted hum on the track (the faulty cable/wiring syndrome mentioned above). It does not require phantom

Figure 4.1 Mic/line level selection on camcorder rear panel (combined with phantom power option)

power, and it's unlikely that you can easily remove the phantom powering from the channel.

If, however, the microphone is part of the viewfinder housing, or a cable runs from the microphone into the camera body without an obvious plug/socket, then the options listed above are not open to you.

Magnetic recording

To date, the majority of camcorders use tape cassettes for recording. Disc based recording is still in its infancy, but is configured along the same lines as disc recording in computers. Moreover, in modern camcorders, the audio and video signals are digitized, so the recording no longer comprises pictures and sound but digital data, irrespective of the medium. In addition, there are also mixers incorporating hard disc recorders for use on location (see Section 22, Sound recordist operation: mixer).

Cassette

The most common system for recording is still the video tape cassette. The tape from the cassette is wrapped around the head drum, and whilst it traverses

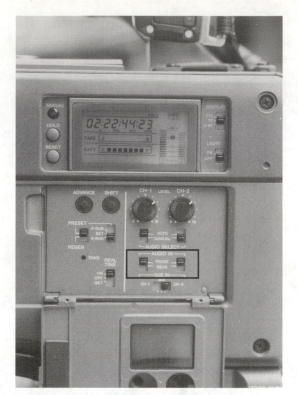

Figure 4.2 Front (on camera) or rear (XLR input) selection for each channel on camcorder side panel

Figure 4.3 XLR connector (with phantom power) for on camera mic

Figure 4.4 XLR socket on camcorder body for mic (usually the camera mic, but you can use it for any mic level input, although phantom power will remain routed via this input)

the drum, the drum spins, such that the recording heads lay down 'stripes' of data on the tape. In analogue systems, the main audio is recorded on separate linear tracks, whilst in digital systems it is more often recorded in the 'stripes' laid down by the head drum.

Do not use the first section of a tape cassette (10–15 seconds) for programme material as tensioning instability may be present. If you do so, you may find that this part of the tape does not produce usable results. Always record a minimum of 30 seconds of line up signal, or, if pushed for time, spool into the cassette before beginning to record your (valuable!) programme material. See also Section 21, Single person operation: shooting; Cassette handling.

Head cleaning
Whatever your recording medium, to maintain sound (and picture!) quality, plus ensuring timecode stability, all recording heads should be cleaned in accordance with manufacturers' directions. On location with today's camcorders, this means you should be using the approved head cleaning cassette.

5 Camcorder: sound levels

Manual or auto

Having plugged your sound feeds you must control the level at which they're recorded. Each track usually has the switchable option of *manual* or *auto* level. Do not rely on this auto function producing the 'correct' level of recorded sound. The auto method of operation is simply designed to increase the channel gain to amplify low level sound, and decrease it for high level sound.

Examples of these two extremes are:

(a) A mic held too closely to a person's mouth will result in the background level falling and rising following the raising and lowering of his/her voice.

(b) Conversely, with a mic at a conventional distance from a person's mouth so that it does not appear in shot, but whilst working in an environment with a varying level of ambient sound, such as a busy road, for example, the overall level will increase and decrease depending on traffic noise, as much as for any variance in voice level.

Both cases will almost certainly render portions of the soundtrack unintelligible and thus, unusable.

Both tracks have individual gain controls associated with their manual position (Figure 5.1). However, do *beware* that most broadcast cameras have a separate gain control for channel one, often on the front of the camera body (Figure 5.2), or on the viewfinder housing (Figure 5.3). This is in addition to, and in line with, the channel gain control on the recorder section. Ensure you locate

Figure 5.1 Channel gain (level) controls

Figure 5.2 Channel one gain control on front of camcorder body

Figure 5.3 Channel one gain control on viewfinder housing

it and check that it's fully turned up (see also Section 20, Single person operation: tracks; Sound level). I suggest you also put gaffer tape over it, to ensure it doesn't get altered accidentally. Each channel gain control must be adjusted to ensure that the correct sound level is recorded. But what is the 'correct' level, and what form of control can we exercise?

Level control and dynamic range

The dynamic range of sound in the outside world can be extreme, especially with aircraft, pneumatic drills and heavy traffic to contend with, if all you want to do is to record speech. Although the ear can cope with this dynamic range, it's unlikely that the signal chain we use can accommodate it to its full extent, although digitization has led to an improvement in the acquisition of a wider range than before. But if we are dealing with television, there is still a poor old transmitter between us and the listener/viewer which cannot fully accommodate the whole range.

Moreover, even were the whole dynamic range transmitted, it's most unlikely that it could be heard in its entirety via the replay/receiver due to the average noise level within most domestic environments, if that is, you're working in broadcasting. However, in order for you to provide optimum results, you *must* understand what is involved in post-production, and the final destination of the finished product – the client/customer/consumer.

Post-production

To take an obvious example, if you are working in a news environment, your recording will almost certainly be used to provide on-air sound without recourse to further processing or dubbing. So it must not exceed the dynamic range of the transmission system, although limiters within the system will ensure no excess level can do any harm. But if you have not adequately controlled your level, those 'downstream' limiters may render portions of your soundtrack muddied or unintelligible, and in a fast turnaround environment, the only time this defect is likely to be noticed is when the material is transmitted – 'Oops, sorry luv!'

If, however, you know that your material will be subject to a dubbing session, then you can leave some of the balance and level decisions to the dubbing editor. To give the editor as much choice as possible, it's best to provide both sufficient level, and as wide a dynamic range as is practical, working within the parameters of your recording format.

Thus, in an ideal world, to competently record sound you need to control the amplified level from the mic via a fader, and to have an indication of the signal strength that you are recording.

Limiter

On some broadcast equipment, a red light on the recorder indicates when the sound level is excessive, and that a limiter is functioning. In order to prevent too high a level of sound being recorded, an automatic cut-off prevents the signal rising above a certain level. A good limiter should act like a 'soft buffer' for incoming sound over this level, and not have too hard a cut-off. Thus, if the incoming sound is only just over the optimum level occasionally, the limiter will gently prevent an audible overload, and its red light will flash temporarily. However, if you drive it too hard, with excessive sound levels, the red light will be on almost permanently, and the sound will almost certainly be distorted.

Caution
Many DV cameras do not have a limiter in the audio chain when used in manual, although there is one in circuit when used in auto. Therefore, incoming sound at too high a level will be subject to distortion, if you do not correctly monitor and adjust your input.

Dolby encoding (noise reduction)

This is a deliberate alteration or 'enhancement' (pre-emphasis) to higher frequencies within the *analogue* sound signal before it's recorded, designed to overcome possible losses in quality in the record chain. Amplifier circuitry produces a certain amount of noise (hiss), which increases with the level of amplification applied. The signal carried by the circuit needs to be significantly greater than this background noise, and you will often find a Signal to Noise Ratio (SNR) figure quoted (in decibels) to indicate the level of noise compared to signal you may expect from a piece of equipment. Obviously, the higher the figure, the better!

Unless otherwise requested by production, the Dolby NR facility should always be selected. On Beta SP equipment, the insertion of the SP tape cassette automatically switches Dolby NR in circuit, regardless of the switch position. The sound is decoded upon replay (but not in all camcorders, especially Beta SP). Digital camcorder systems do not use Dolby encoding.

6   Camcorder: sound metering

The recorder normally has a couple of meters, one for each track, which indicate levels and/or numbers, and wiggle in time with your sound input/s. But can you rely on them to provide you with useful information? Certainly not, unless you're also listening on headphones. A wiggling meter simply indicates a varying level of noise being recorded on that track. Whether it's the sound you want, or spurious noise being generated by your timecode circuitry, mobile phone or RF interference, can only be determined by listening.

Unfortunately, the quality of meters on camcorders often leaves a lot to be desired. Historically, they were volume unit (VU) meters, and invariably one of the cheaper components. However, since they were sited in such a way that they were unreadable whilst the cameraman was operating, they were rarely used as the primary source of level indication. And when a recordist was in charge of the sound, he/she almost always used a broadcast standard mixer, with quality onboard monitoring, usually a PPM.

Nevertheless, a professionally specified meter does provide an indication of the level of sound being recorded, and can help you judge whether it's sufficient or excessive, providing you understand the nature of the display.

(a)   Volume units (VU), measuring power as opposed to voltage, tend to be frequency dependent, prone to over-reading low frequencies (Figure 6.1). They track the average sound level, but do not accurately register the peaks, and are prone to overshoot. The cynical sound recordist will tell you that VU stands for 'virtually useless'. The zero of the scale is approximately equivalent to halfway between five and six on a PPM, and you'll see that the portion of the scale above zero is marked in red. Do not let your recording level go beyond the mid-point of the red portion of the scale (and this is assuming some degree of overshoot). Normal conversation should be reading from below −5 to no more than −2 or −1 (minus is the black part of the scale below zero. And −2 and −1 are not marked as such, you simply estimate their position).

(b)   Bar graph meters (Figure 6.2) tend to be similar to the VU meter, some with the same numerical scale. But others (Figure 6.3), usually on the newer DV camcorders, have a different numbering system (in decibels).

Figure 6.1   VU meter

Figure 6.2 Bar graph meter with VU-style dB scaling (running horizontally)

Figure 6.3 Bar graph meter on more recent camcorders with dB scaling (running vertically)

When using this scale you must keep your sound level from approaching 0 (zero) too closely (imagine it as the 'lid' on a box, once you reach it, you cannot put any more signal – i.e. record a higher level – into it), especially if you are using a DV camcorder, which almost certainly doesn't have a limiter in circuit on manual operation. Although they still operate in a similar fashion to the VU meter, their response to peaks, notably on broadcast models, has been improved.

(c) Peak programme meter (PPM) (Figure 6.4). For many years, the *de facto* standard used in British broadcasting. I have yet to find one on a camcorder, but most broadcast mixers have this type of meter. As the sound level increases, the needle swiftly moves up the scale, but has a slow 'decay' time (damping), thus helping you register the peak sound level. Your highest level should not go beyond 6 on the scale. Normal conversation (interviews, etc.) should reasonably register between 3 and 4, and definitely not peak above 5 (unless the shouting starts!).

Meter summary

There are no obvious similarities between the metering systems, but for those of you with a technical background, in the UK, zero level tone is set to level four on a PPM, and to minus four on a VU meter. Thus, these levels can be taken as equivalent, and are close to the visual mid-point of each meter's scale.

Figure 6.4 PPM. There is a 4 dB change in level between the markings on a PPM scale. Just to be difficult, some models may have a 6 dB range between 0 and 1, and between 1 and 2, you'll need to check the specifications. It is generally agreed that programme material should be kept to within a range of 20 dB, and not exceed 26 dB.

In the case of the bar graph mentioned above, there are differing opinions as to the 'correct' level. (Since the top of the scale is 0 (zero), numerals below this value should have a minus sign in front of them, as they indicate relatively lower degrees of level (in decibels), although the minus sign is not normally indicated on the bar graph LCD display on the camcorder.) Many recordists opt to set tone to register −20 on the scale, in order to leave sufficient 'headroom' for unexpected peaks, and some set it even lower at −22 or −24. It should certainly not be set higher than −18 (see also Section 22, Sound recordist operation: mixer; Limiter).

So, before we start recording, we can utilize the meter to indicate if what we're hearing is of a reasonable level. Hence those well-worn questions such as, 'Tell us what you had for breakfast.' In fact, you simply need to keep people talking until you've established a sound level that sounds right, and doesn't distort. I'd advise you to experiment with levels before you arrive on location, especially if you're unfamiliar with equipment (see Section 20, Single person operation: tracks, levels and practical exercise (c)).

Viewfinder indication
All camcorders I've seen can display a rough indication of sound level in the viewfinder. It usually takes the form of a series of 'blocks', or a line of varying length, at the bottom of frame. Although it's likely to be fed from the metering circuitry, do not rely on it for accuracy, and *always* monitor on headphones.

Auto tone
Many modern camcorders provide a line-up tone when switched to bars with the camera mic position selected (this facility may be turned on/off from the menu). Whilst this provides a high pitched noise at the beginning of the tape, it doesn't help you record the correct level from your mics on location, nor does it give the VT editor any reliable guide to the subsequent level of your recorded sound, since you're unlikely to be using a mixer if you've used the camcorder's tone.

Line-up
It is standard practice to record at least 30 seconds of bars and tone at the beginning of each cassette. These test signals indicate video and audio levels for the subsequent editing process, and have the added advantage of 'getting past' the first section of the cassette which may have tensioning instability (not a problem with disc based recording systems), which would adversely affect the first few seconds of sound and pictures.

Technical: in the UK, the standard line-up check signal uses a fixed frequency tone, generated by an oscillator to give 1 kHz at 1 mW, fed into 600 ohms, and this is referred to as 'zero level'. The equivalent meter settings for this signal are: four on a PPM, minus four on a VU and −18 or −20, or sometimes −24 (depending on mono or stereo deployment, see Section 30, Stereo: mixer; Levels, and also on programme content, e.g. speech or music) on a bar graph meter.

7 Camcorder: external facilities

Sound monitoring

Most camcorders have a small loudspeaker, usually sited on the side panel to be adjacent to the operator's ear when the camcorder is being used hand-held (i.e. on the shoulder). Close to the loudspeaker is an associated volume control (normally labelled monitor), and there may also be another volume control beside this labelled alarm (Figure 7.1). When headphones are plugged into the jack socket (Figure 7.2), the sound feed to the loudspeaker is cut. The volume control/s now affects the level fed to the headphones via the jack socket. There may also be a switch to select either one of two sound feeds (PB or EE) for the loudspeaker/headphone monitoring.

These monitoring controls do not affect the record level, but you must set them at the beginning of the day so that, via your headphones, you may accurately judge the subsequent recorded levels and ensure the consistency of your work (see Headphone monitoring volume control below, and also Sections 12 and 13, Mics: practical listening exercises). Before adjusting your sound levels, you may have to check the position of the front camera operational panel, to ensure the camera's St/by (or VTR) mode is selected.

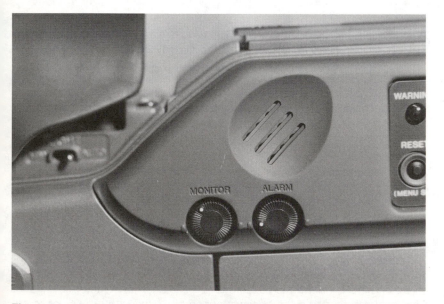

Figure 7.1 Monitor and alarm volume controls sited below the camcorder's onboard loudspeaker. When headphones are plugged into the camcorder the feed to the loudspeaker is cut and these rotary faders then adjust the headphone volume. Unplugging the headphones restores the feed to the loudspeaker

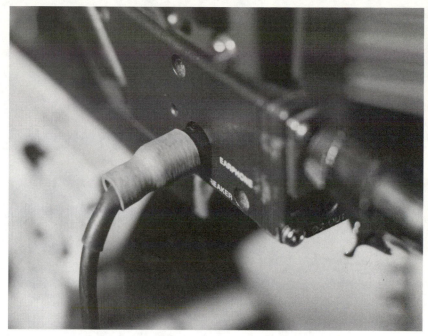

Figure 7.2 Headphones plugged into mini-jack socket on camcorder body

Noise on monitoring circuit

Since your only guide to the quality of the sound you record is via the monitor circuit, you will naturally take great care whilst listening to it to ensure that there is no appreciable interference or other undue noise discernable. However, it is possible for this circuitry to develop a fault, for example an intermittent earth connection, which can generate a hum or buzz which is easily heard on your headphones. Worse still, if you record and replay the tape in the camcorder, the noise is still present, although it is only in the monitoring circuit, and not actually on the tape.

On location, the only way to check that this fault has occurred is to carry a test tape (see also Section 34, Pre-location equipment check; Test tape) which you know has a perfect signal. Put it in the camcorder and see if the noise is now present on replay. If it is, you can be reasonably confident that it is only the monitoring circuit which has the fault, and that the recording is clean. But make a note on the cassette labels that the results should be carefully checked for unwarranted noise. Ensure the camcorder is thoroughly checked before its next operational assignment.

Playback or E to E

Some broadcast camcorders give you a choice of monitoring sound off tape (playback, PB) or E to E (prior to recording on tape) (Figure 7.3). Monitoring PB

Figure 7.3 Playback/EE selection switch for monitoring

ensures a certain amount of confidence in the recorded sound, but it's delayed by roughly a quarter of a second, thus rendering it almost unintelligible, especially as you can probably hear the direct speech as well in most working environments. Worse still, if it has been Dolby encoded, and you're hearing an undecoded replay, the quality will seem overly 'brilliant' – bright and compressed. (This is the case for in-camera review/replay from Beta SP camcorders – also note – with the recorder correctly lined up, the PB level is higher than the recorded level, when monitoring locally, and can thus give you a false impression of your sound levels.) Most recordists opt to use EE monitoring, the sound that is about to be recorded, but it is advisable to check the off-tape recording at every break.

Headphone monitoring volume control

I haven't yet seen one that is adequately protected from accidental knocks or tweaks (Figure 7.1), and you *must* check its position regularly. Set it at the beginning of the day (before you go on location) so that you're monitoring your sound at a comfortable/practical level, and make a note of its position (not the same for all headphones, as their impedance varies from one model to another). Since you're reliant on your headphones to consistently monitor sound levels, you must be vigilant that this control is not altered, unless the ambient noise level intensifies significantly on location.

However, you must also ensure that the level at which you are monitoring does not become audible to anyone else on location, in other words, you don't want any 'sound leakage' emanating from your headphones. Quite apart from the danger inherent in the risk of damage to your hearing if you listen at too high a level for a protracted period, you also run the risk of unnerving the contributors if they can hear any external 'noises off'.

Alarm

Most broadcast cameras have an alarm function which flashes the red cue (tally) light, and sends an intermittent tone in sync with the flashes, to the monitoring chain. Thus, if the associated volume control is turned up, you will hear this in your headphones/on the recorder's loudspeaker. In either case you'll almost certainly find it extremely distracting and, if it becomes activated during recording, it could all too easily cause consternation amongst the contributors (similar to your listening level being too high), bringing the proceedings to a grinding halt. Most operators, therefore, have its level turned down to zero.

Tape/alarm warnings

Possible problems in several functions produce alarm signals, and you must refer to your camcorder handbook for precise information. Common warnings are:

- Battery voltage low
- Tape end imminent
- Tape slack – wind/spool the cassette to correct tension
- Humidity – damp, or moisture on the head drum
- RF – signal not being properly recorded, head to tape contact problem, possibly a head clog
- Servo – tape not lacing or transporting correctly

LCD display

The most prominent feature of the camcorder's LCD display (Figure 7.4) is usually Timecode (see Section 33). It may also display an indication of the tape/alarm warnings listed above. Most digital camcorders also have bar graph (see Section 6) sound metering and a battery level indication. The latter has proved notoriously unreliable in the past on several models of camcorder, and should not be relied upon unless you have tried and tested the individual camcorder/battery combination for yourself.

Other information displayed depends on the software available with each camcorder. Among the options that could be included are items such as menu driven function switching for the record section, editing and/or data flag insertion, and storage of several seconds' worth of sound and pictures which may be made available to the recording medium when you press *record* (for a comprehensive list of what's available, or how to install and operate it, refer to the camcorder handbook).

Camcorder recording operation

On broadcast camcorders starting and stopping the recorder can be achieved by pressing the *record* button on the lens servo package (Figure 7.5), the usual

Figure 7.4 The timecode display is at the top of the LCD screen, and usually larger than the other information displayed

Figure 7.5 Record run (VTR) button on lens

method for most operations, or pressing the button on the front of the camera body (Figure 7.6). The last five seconds (approximately) of recorded material can be reviewed (and the tape accurately reset to start recording at the end of that material) by pressing the Ret (return) button (Figure 7.7) on the lens servo package.

Further recorder controls can be found on the top rear of the camcorder (Figs 7.8(a),(b)). They will not operate whilst recording, but otherwise perform the obvious replay and spooling functions, and the material can be viewed in the viewfinder, or via a monitor (except Beta SP, see playback adapter below). On some digital camcorders editing functions are also associated with these controls.

Eject
The tape eject facility is usually situated on this control panel on broadcast models.

Playback adapter
Beta SP camcorders will only replay material via the viewfinder and onboard sound monitoring. To display colour pictures and sound via a monitor/loudspeaker, a playback adapter is required.

Figure 7.6 Record run (VTR) button on the front of the camcorder body

Figure 7.7 Ret (return) button on the lens servo housing

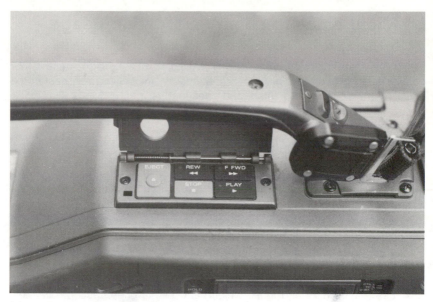

(a)

(b)

Figure 7.8 (a) Recorder operational controls on the camcorder top panel; (b) recorder controls protected, leaving the eject button accessible

8 Mics: types in common location usage

Out of the many different types of mic available, we're going to restrict our consideration to two basic pick-up characteristics, mics that 'hear' best in the direction in which they're pointed, and ones that hear equally in all directions. These are the ones most commonly found on location, and may be considered the workhorses of any professional kit.

Polar response

Most professional microphones are packaged together with a leaflet outlining their operational characteristics, and this may include a polar diagram (unless it's an omni-directional microphone, which rarely does these days). More often than not, the polar diagram is a graphic outline of the pick up characteristic of the microphone, and although it's displayed in two dimensions on paper, it should always be considered in three dimensions when applied to the microphone's operation. Thus, for the mics which we intend to use, those mics which hear equally in all directions – omni-directional – have a spherical polar response (Figure 8.1); and those which hear best in one direction – cardioid – have a roughly heart-shaped polar response (Figure 8.2). The latter response will be frequency dependent, and this should be indicated on its polar diagram, since gun mics, through their design limitations, tend towards an omni-directional response at low frequencies.

Frequency response

If a mic is packaged with a leaflet outlining technical characteristics, it will almost certainly indicate its frequency response. If a mic is expected to emulate

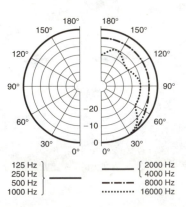

Figure 8.1 Polar diagram of an omni-directional mic (Courtesy of AKG Acoustics, USA)

Polar Response

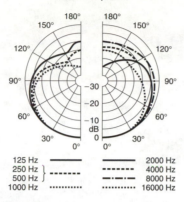

125 Hz ——— ——— 2000 Hz
250 Hz ⎫
500 Hz ⎬ - - - - - - - - - - - - 4000 Hz
1000 Hz ·········· 8000 Hz
            ·········· 16000 Hz

Figure 8.2 Polar diagram of a cardioid mic (Courtesy of AKG Acoustics, USA)

the frequency range and sensitivity of normal human hearing, the graph representing the mic's response should be as close to a straight (horizontal) line as possible, between 20 Hz and 20 kHz (Figure 8.3). Nevertheless, although a straight line is to be desired, operational considerations may necessitate alternatives. For example, you would expect to find that a gun mic should have a switchable bass cut giving a decrease of between 4 and 10 dB at around 50 to 100 Hz, and this in all probability will be indicated by a lessening of response to these frequencies on the graph. However, this facility not only helps directional capability in the case of the gun mic, but also lessens handling noise, and can reduce unwanted rumbling from sources such as traffic.

Gun mic: directional

The gun (or shot gun, or rifle) mic (Figure 8.4) is arguably the workhorse of location sound recording. It hears best along its axis, in other words, the direction in which it's pointing. Its barrel is slotted (interference tube), and this creates a phase differential for sound arriving off axis, resulting in varying amounts of cancellation (see also Section 2, Sound measurement; Phase).

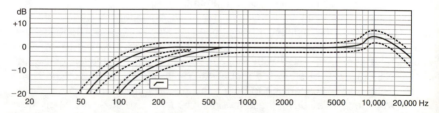

Figure 8.3 A typical frequency response for a capacitor mic, showing bass cut (Courtesy of Georg Neumann GmbH, Berlin)

Figure 8.4 Gun mic

The longer the barrel, the more discriminating the mic is in rejecting off-axis sound, but since sounds have varying wavelengths, the discrimination is also frequency dependent, and most effective for wavelengths shorter than the barrel length, so at long wavelengths, low frequencies, the mic behaves as if it were an omni.

It's a condenser mic (see Section 37, Mics: technical information and operational summaries), and its 'electronic ear' (Figure 8.5) needs a voltage supplied in order to hear anything. The signal generated by the capsule must also be amplified, and the power necessary for these facilities is normally provided via the mic cable (see Phantom powering below). You may prefer to specify the option of running off a dry cell in the housing when ordering/ purchasing one for location use, since not every camera/recorder provides phantom power on both mic inputs. If the mic has no other power option, you're limited to using it with equipment that can provide such power. However, be careful as it's inadvisable to leave a dry cell *in situ* for long periods of time if phantom powering is the norm, in case it leaks or decays, ruining a very expensive piece of equipment!

Whilst you get what you pay for, gun mics designed for broadcast use arguably provide the highest quality sound. However, you do need to take certain care when using them. This design of mic is susceptible to handling noise, and should be used with the correct mounting to function efficiently. Figures 8.6(a) and (b) show the mounting cradle often associated with these mics, using rubber suspension to help minimize unwanted vibration.

Nevertheless, even using these mounts, you must exercise care when moving the mic. You may hear rumbling, should you attempt to reposition the mic too quickly, or rattling caused by the mic hitting the interior of the windshield

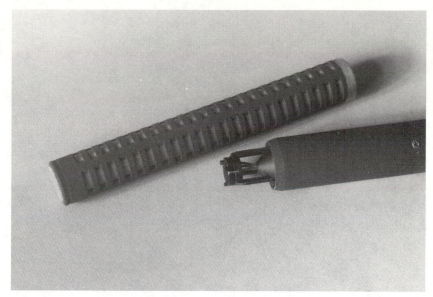

Figure 8.5 A broken gun mic, showing the interference tube and position of capsule in the housing

housing the mounting. You will need to gain skill in order to successfully handle the mic on a pole/boom, although you're unlikely to face this problem whilst engaged in single person operation.

Care must be taken not to work the mic too close to the mouth, as condenser mics are prone to popping, the wind blast on the capsule from heavily accented 'p' and 'b' sounds (and to a lesser extent 'd', 'k' and 't'). It is designed for more distant work (from the sound source). They may also give trouble in damp/wet conditions (fizzing and spluttering), although windshields can help, up to a point.

The onboard camera mic is often of this type, so care must be taken if you are relying on it to provide broadcast sound, as opposed to guide track. From its position on the camera, it is prone to pick up any zoom handling and/or servo noise, so you must avoid accidentally knocking it whilst operating (more likely when the camera is hand-held).

Reporter's hand-held (stick) mic: omni-directional

The reporter's hand-held mic (Figure 8.7), is a dynamic omni-directional mic, which works on the moving-coil principle (see Section 37, Mics: technical information and operational summaries). There are omni-directional condenser mics available, but for location work, I'd advise against them.

Since no signal amplification occurs within the mic, its output is lower than that of condenser mics, and thus it's considered less sensitive. It nevertheless

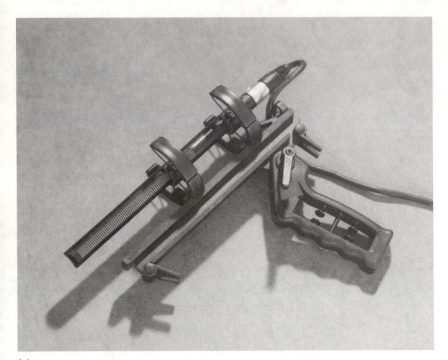

(a)

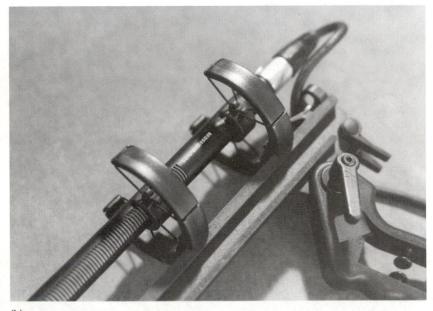

(b)

Figure 8.6 (a) Gun mic in mounting cradle; (b) gun mic in detail

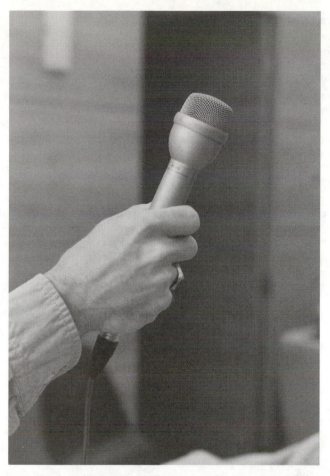

Figure 8.7 Omni-directional stick mic

produces good quality sound (good frequency response), and is an extremely rugged design, standing up to rough handling. Thus it's an ideal mic for hand-holding, and many reporters prefer to have something in their hands, such as the mic, when they're doing their PTCs (the stereotype is mic in one hand, clipboard in the other).

It can also be used very close to the mouth, to provide a good signal-to-noise ratio, and is unlikely to suffer from popping. Partly due to its rugged construction, and since it doesn't require power, it will continue working in adverse conditions when the rest have stopped. For this reason, I would always carry one of these mics as a reliable standby.

Clip (personal) mic: omni-directional[1]

Works on the electret principle (see Section 37, Mics: technical information and operational summaries), which allows for a very small mic capsule (Figure 8.8) ideal for attaching (via pin or clip) to people's clothes, and lending itself to relatively easy concealment. Like the gun mic, it too needs power for signal amplification, provided via phantom power, or a dry cell in the barrel connector (Figure 8.9). The phantom power supply should override the dry cell, which, as already mentioned, should not be left in place if it's likely to remain unused for long periods of time, plus it adds that little bit of extra weight to the connector.

Nevertheless, its small size and weight makes it a favourite for single person operation, as it's so easy to carry. Its sound quality is best described as average (frequency response lacking in bass) and its quality and bass response rely on the proximity effect of clipping it close to the body (gaining some extra bass from the resonance of the chest cavity). By their design, these mics need to be placed within approximately four to eight inches from the subject's mouth. However, people rarely stay absolutely still whilst talking, so beware a turn of the head which results in severely off-mic sound.

Since they are omni-directional, in theory it doesn't matter how they are orientated, and you sometimes see them clipped upside down on contributors (Figure 8.10(a),(b)). Depending on the design of the mic, it is possible that this helps protect the capsule from wind blasting, but I'd advise you to always listen to the output before finalizing your decision on the exact orientation of the mic. If the mic is in shot, it may be that anything other than 'right way up' could prove visually distracting. Alternatively, as far as appearance goes, depending on the style of the mic clip, upside down or even sideways may enable you to make a neater job of routing and concealing the cable.

However, should you need to use a windshield, it's far more likely to drop off an upside-down mic, and once it hits the ground it seems to completely disappear (that's another great time-waster on location, hunt the missing windshield: moral, always carry a spare). Whilst on the subject of windshields, because of their size, the use of clip mics outdoors is often restricted by windy conditions. To be effective, a Dougal-style windshield needs to be large enough to absorb the wind energy encountered. This makes it impractical for clip mics, and the windshields supplied with them tend to be overwhelmed by wind speeds in excess of 10 mph (see also Section 18, Single person operation: specific location scenarios; Wind noise).

These topics are more fully discussed in Section 11, Mics: use of clip mic for seated interview.

M/S

See Section 29, Stereo: mics and placement

---

[1] Directional clip mics are available, but rarely used, and unlikely to turn up in a location kit.

Figure 8.8 Omni-directional clip mic

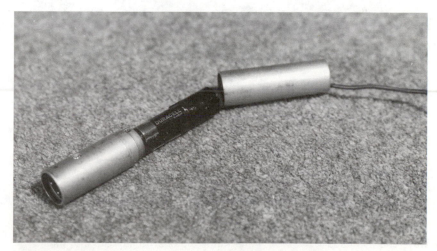

Figure 8.9 Dry cell in barrel housing (to power mic if no phantom power is available)

Figure 8.10   (a) Clip mic in a good operational position

Phantom powering

Condenser mics used in broadcasting are normally capable of being powered via the mic cable. This is known as phantom powering, and it is nominally 48 V. 'Phantom' means that this power used to activate the capsule and/or onboard amplifier should not affect the mic or the audio signal it produces in any other way. The mic usually has a 'P' in its model number to indicate that this is the case (see also Gun mic, and Clip mic above).

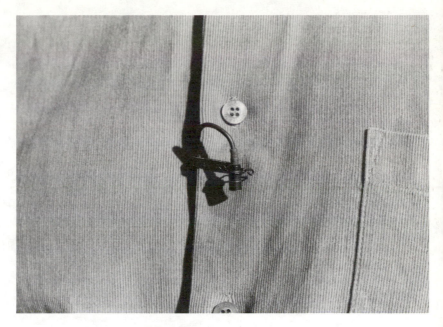

Figure 8.10 (b) Clip mic upside-down

T-power

One point to be wary of is hiring older location gun (condenser) mics that have T-powering (also called A–B powering, or modulation lead powering), normally indicated by a 'T' in the model number. They also obtain their power via the mic cable, but in the range 9 to 12 V. Thus, they are often supplied with their own power supply unit (dry cell/s in a small metal box with XLR input and output). If not, most portable mixers may be switched from P to T to provide the power. *Do not* make the mistake of plugging this mic in with P power (48 V) selected (especially vulnerable to accidental switching if connecting to the rear camcorder input), as you will almost certainly damage its capsule.

9 Mics: cables and radio

A sound cable needs to be as 'transparent' as possible to the signal it's carrying. Hopefully, you won't be required to undertake very long cable runs, but as you can imagine, the output from a microphone is pretty small, and if you have losses or interference brought about by your cable and/or its connectors, it spells extremely bad news.

Balanced line
Put simply, a balanced signal path is one which has the two signal legs (live and return) separated from the earth (screen). A properly screened cable will greatly assist in the reduction of interference (induction) from other sources (Figure 9.1).

To further assist the integrity of the circuit, many professional cables have two wires for each of the legs, and are constructed in such a way that induced phase differences in the signal path along the cable tend to cancel out. This type of cable is termed star-quad, and will normally have an XLR connector at either end (Figure 9.2(a),(b)). Care should be taken not to accidentally connect a balanced line to an unbalanced one (see Direct inject box below).

Unbalanced line
Uses the screen/earth as the return signal path, and cable ends will only have one inner and one outer connection. An example in common use is the phono plug (Figure 9.3).

Direct inject box
For those occasions when you do need to connect an unbalanced line to your mixer, you need one of the many useful little boxes that are prone to gather in a

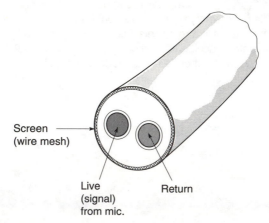

Figure 9.1 Cross-section of balanced mic cable

(a)

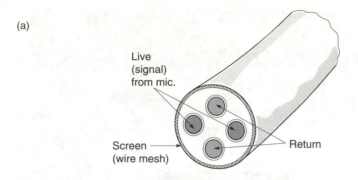

Live
(signal)
from mic.

Screen
(wire mesh)

Return

(b)

Figure 9.2 (a) Cross-section of star quad mic cable; (b) star quad cable with XLR plugs

sound kit called a direct inject box. This is a balance transformer, and has several inputs, often in the nature of jacks and mini-jacks, as well as phono; although you should ensure that whatever one you obtain for yourself has all the requisite types of input socket that you're likely to need in your part of the world. It normally only has one output, an XLR socket, and it may be battery powered. Examples of its use are to connect feeds from semi-pro PA, musical instrument amps, and various domestic audio sources to your equipment.

Straight or curly?

Certain cables are available in curly versions (Figure 9.4), similar to those found on some phone handsets. Whilst at first sight this may seem to be the answer for keeping your cables tidy and flexible, and you might immediately think of it as the solution to working at a variable distance between the camcorder and your mixer, for example, it can in fact pose operational problems:

Figure 9.3 Phono plug

- As the cable extends, it becomes taut, and pulls at either end, which may place undue strain on the connections.
- When one end is attached to the camcorder, the weight of the cable pulls down at the connection, making it heavier to hold and carry.
- Moreover, should it become taut, it could also misalign the camera on its mounting, adversely affecting the framing (Figure 9.5).
- The loops of the cable's curls can snag on objects with which it comes into contact, a tripod leg, for example. In some instances, when the recordist moves around the tripod, the force which the cable's loop is capable of exerting on the tripod locking mechanism has been known to be sufficient to loosen and collapse the leg if it has not been properly locked to begin with.

Plugging
Rather than plug cables directly to sockets, it is good practice to *tie them off*, fairly loosely, beforehand, thus helping to relieve any stress or strain on the connector. If plugging to the camcorder, tie off on the panning handle, or the carrying handle, using a clove hitch (Figure 9.6).

Colours
On complex rigs, it's useful to have a variety of cable colours so that you can distinguish which feed is which at a glance. You can also have coloured glands on the XLR connectors, which may be a preferred option for simply identifying

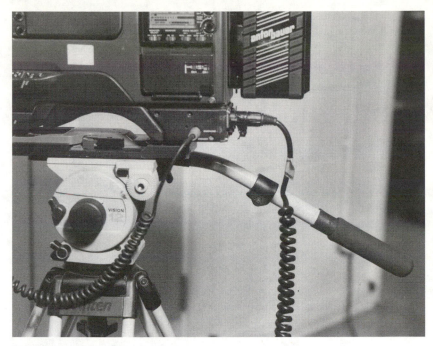

Figure 9.4 Curly lead

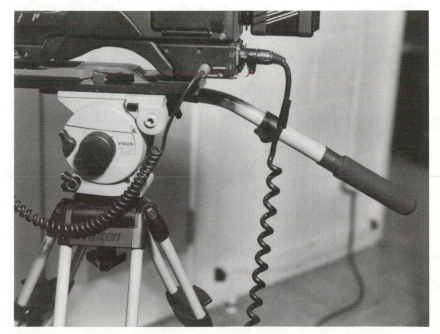

Figure 9.5 Taut curly lead, which can all too easily cause unwanted movement to panning head resulting in misframed shots

Figure 9.6 Cable tied off on pan bar, using a clove hitch

cable ends. Either facility simplifies fault identification and re-cabling due to production changes.

Radio mics

Any mic can be a radio mic. You feed its output into a transmitter, and receive the resultant RF signal at a convenient spot to record it (beside the camera for all intents and purposes) (Figure 9.7).

The most common mic used as a radio mic is the clip/personal, and so it's often mistakenly referred to as a radio mic. To confuse you more, should you order/hire a radio mic, you expect to get a clip mic with a transmitter/receiver combination. Another option available is a hand-held radio mic, which looks similar to a stick mic and has the transmitter built into the handle (Figure 9.8).

Radio mic rules

The rules governing the use of radio mics dictate that for best results you should:

- Ensure that the transmitter does not come into contact with other metal (remove coins, keys, etc. from the pocket, if that's where you put the transmitter).
- **TURN *OFF* ALL MOBILE PHONES.** Do *not* switch them to vibrate/silent instead. They should always be turned off whilst you are recording anyway, but they are especially problematic if used in the vicinity of radio transmitters/receivers.

Figure 9.7 Radio mic transmitter and receiver

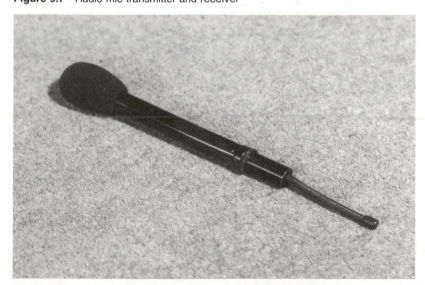

Figure 9.8 Radio hand-held stick mic, with transmitter aerial at base

- Ensure that the transmitter doesn't come into contact with wet surfaces. Wet and damp often hamper RF propagation, and contact with damp skin, a contributor sweating or your hands being wet (with rain!) for example, will almost certainly reduce its range/efficiency.
- Ensure that the transmitter aerial lead is straight. If it's coiled, or otherwise shortened, that too can drastically reduce its range. It must also be kept dry!
- Ensure its 'line-of-sight' to the receiver is unimpaired, especially by metal.
- The receiver aerial often works best when vertical (better still, use a dual aerial – diversity – kit), and should always retain its line-of-sight with the transmitter. Positioning the receiver as high as possible – gaffered to the top of a lighting stand (although ensure the stand is firmly sited, i.e. won't fall or blow over) is the usual quick fix – should help improve the signal path.
- Before recording, check the condition of the batteries in both transmitter and receiver, and change them if in doubt.
- Carefully monitor the recording to ensure no stray clicks, pops, or splats are produced. If there are any, you will have to move the position of one or more of the variables (transmitter, receiver, frequency, batteries, etc. see also Section 35, Fault finding; Intermittent noise). Unwanted noises such as these may be caused by multi-path interference from reflections, so look around for plate glass windows, or water. Large bodies of water can be especially problematic as they can both reflect and absorb RF, depending on your relative positions. Some radio mics have switchable frequencies, enabling you to avoid RF interference, if you're lucky. Even though you have correctly licensed your frequency, that does not stop others illegally using it, and causing you problems.
- At large events, press conferences, etc. there may be other crews legally using the same frequency. If you are working alongside other crews, check with each other as to which frequencies are in use. Always turn your *receiver* on first, and monitor for activity on the frequency. Switching your transmitter on will cause an initial pulse on the frequency, disturbing any ongoing transmissions. If two channels operate on the same frequency (or even close frequencies), the RF signals interfere with each other.

Warnings:

(a) Two transmitters placed side-by-side, even on different frequencies, can interfere with each other.
(b) Using the same channel as another crew does not guarantee that you can utilize their output if their transmitter/receiver is of a different model/manufacturer, due to differences in signal processing between designs.
(c) Legally licensed frequencies in one country may not be legal in another.

- Always replay as much (preferably ALL) of your recording on site to ensure you have no unheard problems.
- There are NO guarantees that it will work 100% of the time.

Were all that not enough to curb your enthusiasm for them, be aware that you'll almost certainly need licences for the frequencies you're using (as mentioned above). If you hire the kit, this should be taken care of, although you must check with the hire company as it's the *user's* responsibility to ensure the kit is licensed. Thus, it's your responsibility to obtain a licence if you own the kit (via JFMG in the UK).

10 Mics: placement with regard to speech

More often than not, sound recordists spend the majority of their time recording speech. The main criterion in recording speech is that it is always *intelligible*. No matter how well lit, framed and composed the pictures may appear, if you can't make out what the person is saying …

The secret of achieving the 'correct' sound is being able to place the correct mic in the correct *position*. The position is all-important, even the world's best mic won't produce good results if it's poorly placed. So, the two decisions you have to make are – which mic/s to use, and how to correctly position it/them.

In the best of all possible worlds, *you* want to *control* the position at all times.

The seated indoor interview
Having said that speech is the bread and butter of a sound recordist's work, let's take a closer look at how best to mic what is probably the most common location subject, the seated indoor interview.

Mic choice
This may be dictated by any extraneous noise that you're unable to control, e.g. in a busy working environment, you could encounter problems with air conditioning, noisy machinery, etc. which forces you to get the mic capsule close to the mouth (see also Section 14, Sound balance and location acoustics). This almost certainly necessitates having the mic in shot, thus making the clip mic the one to use (see Section 11, Mics: use of clip mic for seated interview), being the least visually obtrusive, unless the shot is extremely tight to exclude it. Otherwise, in quieter surroundings, most sound recordists choose the gun mic as the *de facto* standard for this type of work.

If you need to record the interviewer's questions at the same time, you should aim to use the same type of mic for both participants. However, due to the superior quality of the gun mic, if you only carry one in your kit, it's preferable to use it for the interviewee, and one of your others, which may be of slightly lesser quality/sensitivity, for the interviewer; rather than use two clip mics.

Position
The position of the mic is usually governed by the shot size – the tighter the shot, the closer you need to position the mic to the person's mouth to achieve the correct aural perspective. However, if the production requirement is for the shot size to vary, you need to establish a position that gives consistency of sound level. The human ear notices changes in level, and so during an interview, you need consistent sound to ensure edits remain unnoticed. On the other hand, were you to be shooting drama, you may well wish to re-position the mic for each change in shot size in order to match the perspective.

Most recordists operate with the mic on a hand-held pole (Figure 10.1), and an experienced recordist can use this to cover both interviewee and interviewer,

Figure 10.1 Gun mic on pole

as well as subtly altering the mic distance to cope with changes in the level of either voice (see Section 27, Sound recordist operation: pole operation).

Mic stand

Some interviews can be lengthy, and the possibility of fatigue may outweigh the ease of deploying the pole. In these circumstances best results may be obtained by placing a gun mic on a stand.

To allow some flexibility with framing, the mic is usually placed above the top of frame, since changing between MS and MCU doesn't normally alter the headroom excessively. Providing this doesn't cause a shadow problem, or mean that the mic is angled so that it picks up too much extraneous sound, then it's the ideal position (Figure 10.2).

However, constraints on space may mean that you can't always place the stand in an optimum operational position. Moreover, if placed directly on, for example, a wooden or other solid floor surface, it will almost certainly pick up mechanical vibrations transmitted via the floor (although acoustic isolation – thick rubber – should help alleviate the problem).

However, having placed the mic on a stand, and established sound levels before recording, you'll need to ride the gain to cope with variations there-after. People may raise their voice once they begin an interview, especially if they become enthusiastic, excited or overwrought, or they may lower their voice if they imagine they're imparting confidentialities, or expressing their grief.

See also Section 16, Safety; Cables.

Figure 10.2 Gun mic on stand

MCU

MS

Figure 10.3 The mic remains in the same relative position for each of the two shot sizes. This ensures that the sound level will remain consistent and that any subsequent edit will pass 'unheard'

11   Mics: use of clip mic for seated interview

This is often the preferred mic for single person operation, simply due to its size and weight. In an exceptionally noisy environment, it may be the only way to achieve intelligible results, by positioning the mic relatively close to the interviewee's mouth. However, there are several other factors to consider which may influence your choice.

Although their size and weight make them relatively easy to conceal, you'll frequently find that (a) clothing fabrics and fashions may not allow you to do so; and (b) people lacking in television experience may not appreciate the necessity of re-arranging their clothing to accommodate being 'wired for sound'.

Fabrics and fashions

Many synthetic fabrics (especially Nylon) can produce an electrostatic charge, causing clicks and splats to be heard, especially if the fabric comes into contact with the capsule (e.g. should you attempt to conceal the mic underneath clothing). Shiny material can often be slippery as well, and cause the mic clip to slip or skew during the course of an interview. This may cause some variation in the sound, but in all probability the shifting mic will prove more of a visual distraction.

Clothing styles (apart from the fabric problem) can cause headaches with positioning the capsule. A T-shirt for example, forces you to place the capsule too close to the subject's mouth by clipping it on the neckline, unless you can use a pin/clip to position it further down the material. But doing so often pulls at the material, making it an ugly distraction.

Similarly, sweaters/jumpers, etc. may tempt you to place the mic in the optimum position, but not everyone likes you making holes in their (expensive designer-label) clothes using the pin! Various methods have been used to alleviate this problem, including taping the mic on the inside of the material (beware rustling!). Should you consult other recordists, you'll find that each and every one has his/her favourite design/make of clip mic (and accessories) that they use when the need for concealment arises. But even armed with every attachment under the sun in your kit bag, you often have to use all your expertise (and charm) to successfully employ a personal mic in these circumstances (see Making the interviewee comfortable, below).

Lapels are an ideal place to clip the mic (Figure 11.1) (ties as well, depending on the tie material, for those who wear them), and occasionally you'll hear it referred to as a lapel- or tie-mic. Since most of today's clip mics are black, dark clothing is a boon in helping to make them relatively unobtrusive. Nevertheless, you'll still have to put some thought into effectively concealing the cable, so that it won't appear in shot (e.g. poking out from behind the lapel) when the interviewee moves around whilst answering.

Also, if you do clip it to a lapel, beware the interviewee's natural movement, producing off-mic sound. Since the mic is so close to the sound source (the mouth) it's sensitive to an alteration in the distance from the source (see

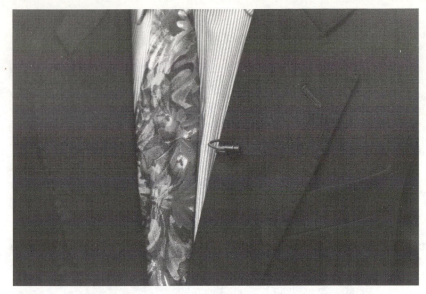

Figure 11.1 Black clip mic on lapel of dark jacket

Section 2, Sound measurement; Inverse Square Law), the most obvious change being when they turn their head. In a 1+1 (one plus one), with the interviewee looking to one side of frame, clip the mic on the side they're facing, although be alert for the possibility that they may start looking around whilst speaking.

If they do move their head and cause the level to vary, you must be ready, and preferably anticipate their movement, so that you can ride the gain in order to compensate. The closer the mic to the subject's mouth (especially in the case of it being clipped to the neck of their T-shirt) the more likely you are to have to constantly adjust the gain for subject movement.

Making the interviewee comfortable
Your first concern, having made the decision to use a clip mic, should be the care you take for the personal comfort of the interviewee. If they are unhappy wearing it, their reaction will show, and adversely affect the quality of the interview.

Experienced interviewees
Experienced interviewees will understand the constraints of the medium, and will almost certainly be wearing suitable clothes. They won't object to undressing in order to hide cables underneath shirts/blouses, or pin, clip or tape the mic capsule under sweaters/T-shirts and the like, or run cables down the leg of trousers/jeans, etc. Television professionals often have clothes altered to

accommodate clip mics and cables, and may well have their own pouch to hold a radio mic transmitter.

They may well suggest how they prefer the mic placed, and if the result sounds satisfactory to you, it's an ideal solution. The well-prepared recordist will have many items in his/her kit bag to help conceal and control the position of both mic and cable (see Last word on cable concealment below). So many factors govern this aspect of using clip mics from clothing to climate and comfort that it's impossible to cover every conceivable combination and permutation you're likely to encounter. However, in order to provide some guidance, you'll find a list of the most useful items in Section 36, Equipment.

The thoughtful recordist will also have carried the mic and cable in his/her inside pocket if the weather is cold, so that the capsule and barrel connector are not cold to the touch!

Inexperienced interviewees

Inexperienced interviewees often need to be put at ease, which should be the director's/interviewer's principal task prior to recording. But the recordist must be sensitive to the atmosphere and/or rapport established with the interviewee, and must be able to act with tact and discretion.

For instance, you cannot expect people to remain motionless during an interview, and items of jewellery (necklaces, chains, pendants, etc,) can easily knock against the capsule, causing unwanted noise. But all too often, the interviewee has worn these very items to look their best, so you must be careful how you frame a request to remove them for the duration of the interview.

Probably the worst case scenario is being faced with a nervous contributor, especially of the opposite sex, and proceeding with the expectation that he/she will allow you to wrestle with their clothing and conceal a mic and cable (and transmitter, if radio mic) and then calmly proceed with a coherent interview. It is almost certainly asking the impossible, so on every job you should be prepared to rethink your approach at short notice and always have a 'Plan B' at the back of your mind.

Last word on clip mics

When they are used, it has too often become the norm to see them in shot. I personally dislike seeing mics in shot, as to me it is visually stating that this is a television interview. It not only destroys the illusion of intimacy the viewer may have achieved during a programme, but also ignores the ideal of invisible technique which we strive to achieve within our craft. If you can, take the time to at least make them unobtrusive; better still, conceal them if at all possible.

Last word on cable concealment

Everybody carries gaffer tape in their kit: it's the first line of 'fix-it' for every conceivable problem. However, do be careful if you use it to fasten/secure cables (from clip mics or earpieces) to clothing. The adhesive on gaffer tape suffers from a tendency to produce a sticky goo if it becomes wet or damp. This is exceptionally difficult to remove from any item/s with which it comes into contact, and if you think that there's any possibility that your contributor might perspire in the 'heat of the moment', for goodness' sake, don't use gaffer!

The most useful 'second line of defence' in the war on errant cables is the use of safety pins. But as I've already mentioned, do be careful that you don't make too big or noticeable a hole in valuable garments, and be **doubly careful** that the cable doesn't pull at the pin/s when the subject moves. Should this happen, you're in danger of it causing too severe a strain on the material, followed by an embarrasing rip or tear (not to mention tears and tantrums). I know, I know, gaffer-taped cable simply pulls away from the material, you can't win 'em all!

Last word!

So, as you see, even in what appears to be a straightforward scenario of one person sitting and talking, there are a great many factors to be taken into consideration regarding the mic and its placement. And there's one vital element I've glossed over, the **time factor**. Too often this overrides all other considerations, and means having to work fast using the minimum of kit.

Mic placement for other subjects is considered in Sections 17, Single person operation: mic placement overview and static operation; 18, Single person operation: specific location scenarios; and 28, Sound recordist operation: multiple contributors.

12 Mics: practical listening exercise (a): mic quality

Listening to mics

So far, we haven't considered the 'listening' aspect of the job. On location, the most practical method is to use headphones (the ubiquitous 'cans' – you'll find more information on them in Section 19, Single person operation: use of headphones). This is the part of the job which, for the best results, you can only gain through experience – listening constantly to your mics. That is the only way you can actually tell that you're obtaining the correct sound.

Practical exercises

But how can you gain this experience? Well, first and foremost, as suggested in the introduction, you will have already been listening to radio and television programmes, as well as countless CDs – in other words, all forms of recorded sound. So hopefully, you'll have at your disposal a radio, a television and a hi-fi/tape/CD player, each with its own loudspeakers, for the purposes of this exercise.

You'll also need the mics you intend to assess, a pole for mounting, and ideally a means of recording the results, preferably a camcorder, or at minimum, a high quality disc or tape recorder. Most importantly you must be able to listen to the mic outputs on headphones (ideally via the camcorder monitoring socket). First, you must establish a 'comfortable' listening level, which is not overly loud. Apart from damaging your hearing by listening at too high a level, on location, if you tend to monitor at a high level, the sound from your headphones will 'leak' out and may disturb your contributors. You must also ensure that your listening level (headphone volume) stays constant once set, as the perceived tonal quality of sound changes with volume. The ear does not have a flat response, and sounds appear to have more bass (and to a lesser extent, more treble) when the volume is increased.

The two exercises, (a) and (b) (Section 13) should be paired and undertaken one after the other. Exercise (a) helps you appreciate the quality of each mic and (b) underlines the importance of mic placement (Figure 12.1).

(a) Mic quality. For this, you'll need one source of high quality sound that can be repeated indefinitely, so I suspect you'll almost certainly pick one of your favourite CD tracks! Ideally, in your listening environment, you want to ensure that the background noise level is low, and that there aren't likely to be any other extraneous noises off that might distract you! At this stage, since we're only interested in the sound from a single source, you need to disconnect/remove the second loudspeaker to obtain the ideal listening conditions. Since you want to listen to the mic output, and not the CD direct, you either need to use closed headphones (if you have a pair) or, especially if you are also familiarizing yourself with a more open pair

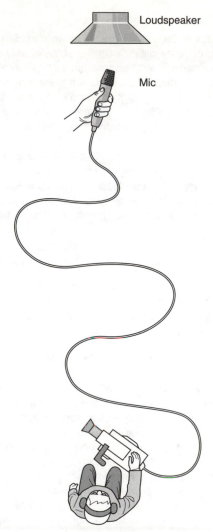

Figure 12.1 Sit as far as is practical from the loudspeaker

for professional use, work as far from the loudspeaker as possible whilst listening. Direct someone else to place the mic for you.

Failing outside help, you could place the mic on a stand and reposition this yourself, or you could mount it on the end of a long pole, and manipulate it from a distance. Neither solution is ideal, however, since either option tends to distract you from the vital task of listening, the latter especially so until you become familiar with handling a pole. Thus, you could all too easily miss the finer points the exercise hopes to demonstrate with respect to mic movement.

Omni

I'll consider omni mics first. In theory, no matter at what angle you place them relative to the sound source, they will pick up the same quality of sound. Try it and see. Keeping the mic capsule in the same place, I'd recommend you start about a foot, 30 cm, from the loudspeaker, does it make any difference to the sound if you angle the body of the mic? You may find there is a very slight difference with some clip mics, although I suspect that's more likely due to it being almost impossible to rotate the mic and keep the capsule in exactly the same spot.

Also move the mic slowly backwards and forwards to and from the loudspeaker, and notice any change in quality as you increase and decrease the gain to maintain constant input to your recorder. Then, keeping the mic gain constant, listen to the drop off in level as you double the distance from the loudspeaker, then double that again, and remember this as best you can for later comparison with the gun mic.

Directional

For this, remove the gun mic from any cradle, mounting or windshield, so that you (or preferably your 'assistant') are holding the barrel close to the base where the cable is plugged. Take care not to cover the slots along the length of the barrel. The first thing you should notice is that compared to the omni stick, it's extremely sensitive to being handled. You can almost certainly detect any slight movement of fingers on the barrel. This underlines the importance of correctly mounting the mic whilst recording.

Start by working the mic about a foot (30 cm) away from the loudspeaker, and, without adjusting the incoming level via the fader, turn the mic in different directions, keeping the capsule in roughly the same position. Obviously, the best pick-up will be when the mic is pointed directly at the speaker, and as it's turned away, you'll find that once it gets beyond about 20° off axis, the level begins to decrease. Depending on the particular mic you're using, you may find its response has an 'edge' which is easy to detect.

Experiment to see (hear!) whether the mic's characteristics are consistent in all three dimensions. In other words angle the mic away from the loudspeaker both in a vertical and then in a horizontal direction (plus any angle you care to try in between) and determine whether the drop off in level is consistent in all three dimensions. This should be the case with any reputable broadcast quality mic, but I have known peculiarities with cheaper versions.

You'll find that mics from different manufacturers have slightly differing directional characteristics. You should also notice that no mic entirely loses or eliminates sound, no matter how you alter its angle relative to the source. Some are better than others at 'rejecting' off axis sound, and many experience an increase in pick-up from the rear, compared to the side. So, if you're unfamiliar with a particular make or model it's always best to evaluate it carefully before taking it on location.

Once you're satisfied with its directional capabilities, keep it pointed towards the loudspeaker and double its distance, then double it again. If you've managed to perform this experiment in a quiet environment you'll be surprised to hear that the level of incoming sound drops off in much the same way as the omni mic at the same distance.

Therefore, do be aware that the gun mic simply discriminates in its acceptance of sound along its axis. The better the design (and usually the more expensive the mic!) the better the directional discrimination of the mic; and to a certain extent, the longer the barrel of the mic, the better the directional discrimination.

The recording

If you have recorded the results, feed both your recording and the original sound via a switch to the same loudspeaker, and alternate between each source. At this stage, listening to the loudspeaker is most important, as this is how the majority of your potential audience will be hearing your efforts. Ask yourself – how 'transparent' does the mic sound – has it introduced any colouration or distortion to the recorded sound – and how has its position affected the recording?

13 Mics: practical listening exercise (b): mic placement and sound discrimination

One ear

This exercise furthers your ability to appreciate the nature of 'one ear' – a mic capsule – substituting for *both* human ears in the real world – the essence of balancing on location. For this you will need two *differing* sound sources about six feet (2 m) apart. I suggest using your radio and television, since you can easily change stations/channels to give you a variety of sounds to experiment with. Set both to deliver as equal a volume of sound as is practical, and mount your mic on a pole.

At this stage you don't need closed headphones, since it's useful to discover how the overall sound direct, versus the sound via the mic/headphones combination, sounds to you as you move your mic, a more true-to-life recording situation. Monitoring and recording your results, as per Section 12, Mics: practical listening exercise (a), start with the mic as far as possible and equidistant from both sources, and move it slowly towards the loudspeaker of one of the sources. Hold it in this position for a few seconds, then move it slowly across to the loudspeaker of the second source and again hold it in position for a few seconds.

Perform this exercise first with an omni and then with a gun mic (if you're recording your results, remember to verbally ident each part of your recording with which mic you're using). When using the gun mic, keep it pointing directly towards the first source for the first part of the move, hold it stationary for a few seconds, then angle it towards the second source before once more moving it across to it and holding it stationary.

Notice how the sound from your selected source becomes more intelligible/clearer the closer the mic gets to it, and the difference between the omni and the gun mic. Working either mic close to one source enables you to virtually exclude all the sound from the other. But, notice how much more control you can achieve with the gun mic via the angle at which it's placed. However, do you always need to cut out as much extraneous sound as this? Don't forget that the secret of using one mic on location is to establish a *balance* between intelligible sound whilst retaining an ambient aural 'flavour' of the surroundings (see Section 14, Sound balance and location acoustics).

You may find it useful to repeat the exercise with the gun mic to determine how it responds at differing angles and distances from each individual source. Try varying the distance between the sources, and adjust your mic position to give an indication of the relative distance between the sources.

The recording

Play back your recording, listening on a loudspeaker, and judge how successfully you've achieved a balance between the two sources. Does it sound exactly as you had expected/intended?

Once more, with pictures

The ideal way to complete this exercise is with a camera and cameraman, during a social occasion (friends round for a day, out on a shopping trip, etc.). Before you have a lot of experience, it's best to work alongside friends, who'll put up with you waving a mic at them. You can work with the mic plugged directly into the camcorder, or via a mixer to the camcorder, but do ensure you monitor the sound feed correctly on your headphones via camcorder or mixer. If time and circumstances allow, try the exercise with both mics.

First agree with the cameraman a sequence of people you're going to speak to, and have him approach each in turn and ask a question (you can always fall back on the hoary old standby 'What did you have for breakfast?' if all else fails). This is the equivalent of shooting vox pops, and is certainly a skill you'll need to acquire if you aim to work in broadcasting.

Once you can keep up with a pre-arranged order for the participants, get your cameraman to approach people randomly, and see how quickly you can get the mic in position so that:

- You can hear intelligible speech.
- The background sound gives the correct aural ambience for your surroundings (and matches the pictures).
- You constantly maintain the correct balance between the two.
- The overall sound level you record is correct.

To make yourself work really hard, see if you can position the mic to hear the question and then reposition sufficiently swiftly to hear the full answer (and without any mic/pole handling noise being apparent). A final word of advice: don't replay the results in front of the others until you've had a look and listen for yourself! Nevertheless, when you do so, the comments you receive can often help further your understanding of other peoples' expectations.

Further listening

Both exercises (a) and (b) should be repeated from time-to-time when you have different mics to test, and to gain confidence in your ability to produce consistent recordings. See also Sections 20, Single person operation: tracks, levels and practical exercise (c); and 25, Sound recordist operation: practical exercises (d) and (e).

14 Sound balance and location acoustics

Sound balance

At each location, you'll be faced with human voices which you want record intelligibly, plus other sounds relevant to the location itself. These form an aural background, and you need to obtain a balance between the two. Otherwise, if you eliminate the background sound altogether (perhaps using extremely close mic technique) the result will probably sound much as if it had been recorded in a studio, whilst the pictures tell a different story.

Ah, the magic of television. Whilst the main concern when dealing with contributors is to record intelligible sound, you also want to match the sound to the pictures. For example, if you interview someone in an open-plan office, you expect to hear phones, conversation, computers, copiers, air conditioning, etc. in the background. The secret is to establish a believable balance between the speech and the background noise.

Moreover, the pictures often assist you when you have extraneous noise, because as long as the source of the noise appears in shot, e.g. traffic when standing at the roadside, then the viewer can tolerate/accept a fair amount of the noise. This is the reason why most television sound – although of high quality in itself – is unacceptable as radio sound (in which you expect a lower background level), since the sound in each medium is doing a different job.

Open-plan office example

However, you still have to judge the level of background sound that's acceptable/desirable. Let's go back to the open-plan office, and listen to the gun mic (on cans, of course). Angle the mic in different directions, and listen to the changing level and quality of the background sound.

If there are conversations, phone calls, etc. they must be kept below the level of intelligibility if you're concentrating on a contributor speaking in front of the camera. In this instance, you must beware of sounds becoming confusing to the listener, as opposed to positively contributing to the aural experience. Once words become distinguishable, the ear/brain will attempt to incorporate them into a coherent whole, and following two unconnected conversations at once is next to impossible with both ears, and completely incomprehensible with one mono mic!

Air conditioning, computer fans, photocopiers, water coolers, etc. all need to be kept to a *constant* minimum. It may not be necessary to completely lose these noises, providing you are confident they won't suddenly change in level. (Phones ringing in the background will only prove a menace if your recording needs to be edited at that point, see Section 15, Recording for the edit; Wildtrack).

This is the secret of using mics, listen to their output and move them around to find the best position to obtain the sound you want. The omni mic lets you balance the sound by varying its proximity to the contributor. The gun mic not only enables you to control the balance of intelligible sound to background noise by its proximity, but also its angle and position help you minimize unwanted noise. It is for you to judge which mic suits your needs, and that of accurately portraying the ambience of the location behind the dialogue.

Location acoustics

Rooms with hard surfaces (e.g. tiled walls, windows) and/or high ceilings usually suffer from over-reverberant sound (especially indoor swimming pools and tiled shower areas in changing rooms, which frequently produce severe echo), possibly making speech indistinct. Using a gun mic may not always lessen the pick-up of unwanted sound, since sounds apparently off-mic may be reflected straight back into the capsule, depending on its position relative to the reflective surface. You can adjust its angle to minimize the effect, but if you're forced to record in this type of location (and beware the spacious board-room) you'll almost certainly need to use close mic techniques, probably necessitating the use of a clip mics. However, if the shot shows the room size, allow some of the 'spaciousness' into the soundtrack.

As already mentioned (Section 2, Sound measurement; Acoustics), soft furnishings, carpets, curtains, even shelves of books, can all help to deaden the acoustics, and these surroundings are more frequently preferred as a setting for location recording.

Voice-over

You may be asked to provide voice-over narration from a presenter/reporter on location, and for this you won't want any hint of location acoustic. Depending on the 'quality' of their voice, a gun mic working relatively close to their mouth is the preferred option, or the stick mic (probably working even closer) if the gun proves unsatisfactory. To help acoustic isolation I've even wrapped curtains, rugs or bedclothes around narrators to achieve the desired result (just so long as they're not claustrophobic!). Listen carefully to ensure they don't rustle their script, and suggest they re-write it if necessary to avoid turning a page (and yes, they may need to use a torch when wrapped in curtains, etc. and you know who they expect to provide one!).

15 Recording for the edit

Having established an acceptable sound balance, you must ensure the level you record remains consistent for editing purposes. You should ask yourself:

- Is the background sound level likely to fluctuate?
- If so, how much?
- Is that likely to prove obtrusive?
- Is there another source of sound likely to cause problems during the recording at this particular location (aircraft, construction, roadworks, etc.)?

You have to anticipate the answers to these questions, but a look around your location before you start recording should help you pin-point any likely sources of unwanted interruptions.

Murphy's Law

Be warned, Murphy's Law operates the moment you start recording (whatever can go wrong, will go wrong), so always be prepared to deal with the unexpected. The minute you run to record, helicopters appear overhead, lawnmowers and hedge cutters race out of hiding, motorcycles scream round the corner, pneumatic drills immediately thunder away, and you, as the recordist, may be expected to ascertain how long any of these interruptions will last. Whilst tact and discretion frequently save the day, there may well be times when you have to proceed with your recording regardless of the noises off, which could leave you facing some tough decisions with respect to the end product. If the sound becomes unintelligible, or you realize that an edit can't take place within a portion of the recording, you must point this out to production and either suggest a re-take, or some covering sound (see Wildtrack below), or even a complete reposition of the item.

An unexpected interruption can also take the form of a change in background noise. Do beware of computer noise, printers, copiers, fridge compressors, air conditioning, etc. as a background constant. Should this noise suddenly cease, you've got a potential editing problem. The best bet is to turn all these devices off, if possible, before you start recording, then at least they can't cease of their own accord (but for goodness sake *remember* to turn them on again before you leave, or you'll not be welcomed back to that location). If in doubt, record a thirty second wildtrack *before* any other activity takes place.

Other noises to beware of are muzak/radios, etc. playing in the background, or any regular noise, like a clock ticking. This type of sound certainly adds to the ambience of the location, but invariably obstructs an edit. So, the only safe way to overcome the problem is to eliminate it altogether. Get the muzak (radio) turned off (see also, Copyright below) and stop the clock. (A word to the wise: by doing this, you may make yourself extremely unpopular. Employees swear they can't work properly without the radio, and the clock is an antique grandfather clock that's been in the family for generations, and has never stopped.

You can guarantee that once stopped, it'll never re-start. Whoever said this job was easy?)

Run to record ... and cut!
When you have started recording, do not let any action commence until you have been running (turning over) for *at least* ten seconds. Similarly, when the action has finished, do *not* cut immediately, but continue to run for a minimum of ten seconds. Whilst these timings used to be mandatory in order for playback machines to stabilize for an edit, they also serve the (more!) useful purpose of giving a sound lead in and run out, in addition to any wildtrack. If there is an ongoing/passing background noise, such as an aircraft, etc. this should be allowed to die away before cutting. Indicate, by pantomiming 'hush', that all on location should keep quiet in these circumstances.

Wildtrack
(Also known as atmos or buzz track, or 'room tone' in the USA.)

How to win friends and influence editors! To help overcome those situations outlined above, one minute of wildtrack can save the day (literally). Record the clock ticking, striking the hour, the bells tolling, the muzak playing (see Copyright below), the builders hammering, etc. This background sound can be added at the edit to reinforce the acoustic atmosphere/ambience, or to help 'sweeten' an edit (i.e. cover the join).

Whatever your location, I would always recommend recording some wild-track. This is especially important if there's a fluctuating level of background sound, even though it's relevant to the location. During an interview, there may be distant traffic, or aircraft noise, but you can bet your boots when an edit is required later, the noise will be at a peak which needs to be sweetened to become unnoticeable.

Whilst recording, be aware of these inconstant noises off, and if and when they peak during the recording. You must then record a wildtrack with the mics in the same positions once you have finished recording the main soundtrack. Whatever the background noise you heard, ensure that you obtain a complete cycle (cars, lorries, trains, planes, helicopters, etc. passing outside). You'll need to be firm, even 30 seconds seems like half an hour, and you *must* ensure that the contributors (and production team) make no noise whatsoever during your wildtrack, for it to be of any use.

Copyright
Whilst a soundtrack of any background noise on location is vital, you should be aware that some sounds, music especially, are subject to copyright. You should indicate to your production team on location that they may need to seek clearance for your wildtrack, and also ensure you make a note on the cassette to alert the editor of a possible restriction in its use. If the sound is subsequently included in the edited mix, it's the production's responsibility to obtain the necessary copyright clearance.

16 Safety

First aid
Everyone who works on location should be familiar with basic first aid. Most employers will send staff on first aid courses at their request, and for freelancers it's worth checking if courses and/or funding are available via professional bodies (see Appendix A).

High sound levels
One hazard which can be cumulative is exposure to excess levels of sound, especially whilst wearing headphones and working in noisy environments. It is all too easy to overlook, but could well lead to a diminution of your hearing sensitivity if allowed to develop. Check the level you're feeding to your headphones, and whether the volume control is always set to maximum. If in doubt, ask a colleague if they think your monitoring level is excessive, and seek medical advice if any doubt lingers.

Accident
If the worst should occur, make sure you have a contingency plan. After administering first aid and alerting the emergency services if necessary, the contact information from the call sheet is vital. In this day and age, no crew should be without a mobile phone.

Pre-location planning
Carefully read and check items on the call sheet. There should be a copy of the hazard or risk assessment form regarding the location/s, or at minimum a note of such items from it that pertain to the crew.

If you are available to recce a location – ensure you list possible hazards and provisions made to address them, for example:

- construction site – hard hat
- chemicals – goggles and other protective clothing?
- water – self-inflating lifejackets
- hospital – batteries, do not use lighting stands or cables

Ensure that responsibility for providing the necessary protection is clearly stated.

Weather – note forecast – but always include provision for inclement conditions.

Facilities – how close/accessible are parking, toilets, food, drink, accommodation?

For a fuller account of planning procedures, etc. see Section 38, Call sheet details.

On location

Rigging

Do not place items in a dangerous position (temporarily resting unsecured on a ledge, steps or stairs, for example, Figure 16.1), and take care when manoeuvring them into confined spaces. If working at height, ensure the stability of the structure (e.g. scaffolding, towers, etc.) together with the proper placement of kicking boards, safety rails, etc. *Do not* carry equipment up and down ladders, but with a second person supervising, raise and lower it tied to a suitable length of rope – a clove hitch (Figure 16.2) is an invaluable knot to learn. If the equipment is heavy, raise or lower it via a pulley and/or hoist.

Handling and carrying

If equipment is an awkward shape, and/or heavy and bulky, do not strain yourself by attempting to move it unaided. *Always* seek trained/experienced help when necessary.

Electrical

Most location equipment is designed to run on batteries, but if you do have to plug in to the mains, use an RCD (Figure 16.3), or equivalent safety device to protect circuitry from equipment failure. Beware that others on site may often plug their equipment (which you cannot always check for safety beforehand) into your socket/s.

Figure 16.1 Do not temporarily place items in unsafe positions (such as this monitor in danger of over-balancing on stairs)

Figure 16.2 Rope tied in clove hitch to camera carrying handle

Cables

Care must be taken when laying cables around a location. This usually entails gaffer taping them in place, especially in areas to which the public have access. If there's even a small gap with cable showing, someone's bound to catch their toe or heel in it, and either injure themselves, or pull over a piece of equipment, thus endangering others (not to mention damaging said equipment). To cover several cables, use rubber matting, and gaffer tape along the edges for best protection.

Do *not* run cables across an emergency exit under any circumstances, but sling or secure them over it if this is their only possible routing.

On *exteriors*, special cable ramps/guards may be necessary/mandatory (especially if crossing a traffic route/road). Firmly encase any cable connections in waterproof covers for additional protection, and do not lay them in crevices, gullies etc. which are likely to become waterlogged in the event of rain.

Shooting

Clean/disinfect earpieces

A sound recordist is often asked to supply earpieces for contributors, so ensure you carry disinfectant wipes to clean them. I have suffered from an ear infection myself through using an earpiece, and I can assure you it's an extremely painful

Figure 16.3   RCD, *always* use this when plugging equipment into a mains supply

experience. Most chemists sell antiseptic cleaning wipes (which can also be used to give your hands a quick wipe when someone turns up on location with a quick snack for the crew!).

It's a wrap
The most dangerous time on location is often during the de-rig, at the end of a working day when people are tired, and in a hurry to get away. *Do not rush*, and do not let others pressurize you into doing so (for example, with claims that a building has to close in five minutes, and the doors will be locked, etc.).

Personal comfort
Keep warm and dry. If you get too hot, you can always take something off, but if you get cold, it's extremely difficult to warm up. Working on location may often involve remaining motionless for long periods of time, in all conditions. Ensure

you have fully waterproof clothing, coat (with hood), over trousers, and footwear to suit the conditions. Carry an extra sweater, plus hat, gloves, etc. and if you're really unsure of what you might face, a complete change of clothing.

Conversely, in hot and sunny conditions, do not leave skin uncovered all day. Beware of exposure to the sun's direct rays, and carry lots of sun tan cream (apply regularly and liberally) and wear a wide-brimmed hat or peaked cap, if practical, together with fully UV protective sun glasses.

Avoid dehydration and a drop in blood sugar level. Keep some 'emergency rations' in your vehicle, chewy bars and a bottle of water and/or cartons of fruit juice, if you prefer. But, do not let their presence encourage you to miss or skimp on having proper meals and breaks during the day. Another life-saver is to have a 'bag of money', i.e. loose change, available in your vehicle for parking and other vital expenses.

Problems

You will often find that, inevitably, there is never enough time to do everything required by the production, and that you are delayed by the most unlikely and unexpected occurrences beyond everyone's control. To help minimize problems that may arise from unforeseen circumstances, insist on scheduled breaks, as well as meals, as they provide a flexible buffer. They also fulfil another function. Bear in mind that much location equipment is heavy to carry; and operational concentration and physical exertion both contribute to fatigue, which can overcome even the most dedicated professionals. If you reach this stage, pressing on regardless can frequently be counter-productive; and in the worst case scenario could lead to a potential safety hazard being overlooked by any or all of the crew.

At all times

Your actions, and instructions to those working with you, the equipment and its operation, **must in no way endanger** the public, contributors, your colleagues, or yourself (Figure 16.4).

Insurance

See Section 39, Insurance.

(a)

(b)

Figure 16.4 (a) When your subject is walking towards you do NOT attempt to walk backwards unaided (b) Always get a second person to guide you (preferably with one hand in your belt) if one shot demands that operation. Otherwise it's a situation that potentially places you, and everyone else around you, in danger.

17 Single person operation: mic placement overview and static operation

(In the following sections under Single person operation, for 'reporter' read reporter/interviewer/presenter/talent/contributor, whichever applies.)

I realize it's an obvious statement, but operating by yourself, you're limited by only having one pair of hands, although an experienced operator will know when the time has come to ask for assistance. However, in this day and age I also realize that, although you may require assistance, the likelihood of getting any is next to impossible, due to 'budget constraints' (you'll recognize the terminology if you've been on a management course).

Thus, as well as being responsible for the sound, you're also responsible for the pictures: lighting, exposure, colour balance and composition. You also have to bear in mind the requirements of the edit, keeping an eye on continuity and subject position, plus you'll probably be expected to remember who said what and when. Again, experience is the only guide as to how much one person can achieve without compromising the intelligibility/fidelity of the recorded sound.

Moreover, working alone with your 'one pair of hands' limits the amount of equipment you can carry. So in this section, I'm assuming that you carry a fairly basic kit, which for the purposes of simplicity, will consist of mics that are plugged straight into the camcorder. More sophisticated techniques, for example, pole operation together with using the mixer, are covered in differing parts of Sections 22–28, Sound recordist operation.

Mic choice and placement

More often than not, time is your enemy, and although the professional within you would prefer to use a gun mic on a stand to acquire the best quality sound, the practicalities involved in carrying it around, setting it up and running the cable safely around the location (ensuring it is firmly secured, using gaffer tape where necessary) may not endear you to everyone, especially not a first-time client!

Hence, many single operators simply clip a radio mic on the person in shot. It's relatively quick and easy, slips neatly into your pocket for carrying between locations, and there aren't any cables trailing around your feet. But please refer to Section 9, Mics: cables and radio, which outlines possible pitfalls and limitations inherent in RF transmission, and Section 11, Mics: use of clip mic for seated interview, for a consideration of the pros and cons of clip mics.

Remain stationary

As often as not, location sound recording involves contributors in static positions, seated or standing in frame. As a single person operator, this is bound to be in your best interests, as the less you have to move around from pillar to post with equipment, the better. Hence, if you are asked for advice by production on the issue, I suggest you point out to them that a static position invariably proves to be the quickest in terms of set-up (and de-rig) and the most reliable and efficient in respect of sound (and picture) acquisition for single person operation.

Unfortunately, many producers/directors become entranced by the notion of 'moving pictures' and frequently endeavour to construct shots featuring the reporter and/or the camera moving as well. Whilst there are undoubtedly occasions when shot development can prove effective, simply moving for the sake of it should be discouraged wherever possible. All too often the problems thrown up by a move can prove detrimental to mic placement, and/or involve extra time spent co-ordinating walking, talking, panning, tilting and zooming, etc. and in the long run only lead to sub-standard results. If you can, suggest a compromise whereby you shoot at least one take of the 'stodgy' static shot, and then, if time allows, go for the all-singing, all-dancing, bells and whistles alternative.

Piece to camera

The most straightforward situation you are likely to encounter is one person speaking to camera (or in other words, the reporter talking directly to the viewer), the PTC. However, although you only have one person in vision whose speech is being covered by one mic, you should *always* use both sound tracks, plugging the main mic into channel one, and selecting your camera mic to channel two. Whilst not totally failsafe, this method of operation does provide a certain amount of back-up in case of unforeseen problems.

If the reporter is sufficiently experienced in mic handling technique, you could ask him/her to hold the gun mic at waist level (preferably out of shot). In most instances, this should provide you with intelligible dialogue against the aural background, unless you're in a noisy environment. In these circumstances, you may find a clip mic positioned closer to the mouth (than the gun mic) produces a satisfactory balance between dialogue and background, unless the surrounding noise is particularly severe.

In which case, you are going to have to position a mic capsule much closer to the reporter's mouth, which almost certainly means a mic appearing in shot. And, whilst I, as a cameraman find this intrusive, I should point out that there are occasions when being unobtrusive is not necessarily what's required, regardless of the background noise level. Certain television stations insist on their reporters using a stick mic complete with channel logo (Figure 17.1). Woe betide those of you who don't get it in shot!

However, if you don't have the logo foist upon you, your choice may simply be aesthetic, which mic looks best? We've already suggested that the stereotypical reporter has a stick mic in one hand and a clipboard in the other, and this could well be the time you put it to the test. Or you may prefer to use the gun mic, although since it's prone to popping especially at close quarters, I would only suggest it as more or less the last resort. Moreover, since gun mics are prone to handling noise, you are now relying on the reporter having the necessary mic handling experience, and you must always remember that once the mic is in somebody else's hands, so is your reputation for sound acquisition!

Figure 17.1   Stick mic with logo (make sure it's in shot!)

Should the background noise level be varying constantly, reduce the gain of the camera mic on channel two, especially if you're using a DV camcorder, in order to accommodate any overload and peak distortion, should events become extremely loud. Although, if this does prove to be the case, in all likelihood the reporter's words will be lost/unintelligible on either channel, occasioning a retake.

One plus one

When faced with two people, you would normally use one mic apiece, feeding one to channel one and the other to channel two. Depending on what you have in your kit, you may use:

- two clip/radio mics
- one clip and a gun or stick mic
- a gun and a stick mic.

In conventional interview situations, single person operation almost always dictates the first option, unless you only have one radio mic, in which case use a cabled clip mic for the reporter beside the camera, or a cabled stick mic, if you don't have two clips. If their questions aren't vital, you may pick up sufficient guide sound from the on-camera mic, which should be selected to channel two if you are only using one radio/clip mic on the interviewee.

If the questions are vital, and you only have one clip mic, use a gun mic, which is best on a stand (see Stand mic, below) for the interviewee and place the clip mic on the reporter. If the stand/gun mic option is too unwieldy/time-consuming, use the clip mic for the interviewee and have the reporter hold the other mic (gun or stick), but do ensure that they have sufficient experience to hold it correctly. Fortunately, the majority of aspiring professionals will welcome guidance in this matter (but will probably forget everything you've said once you start recording.).

If both contributors are together in vision, the most unobtrusive solution is almost certainly to use a radio/clip mic for each. But if you only have one in your kit, place the radio/clip mic on your interviewee (selected to channel one) and give the stick mic to the reporter to hold (channel two). Otherwise let the reporter use the stick mic in the time honoured fashion of moving it between themselves and the interviewee (on channel one), and select the camera mic to channel two, but be especially vigilant monitoring the channel one input for suitable level and intelligibility. Visually, you may need to offer advice and guidance to your reporter in order to avoid too distracting an arm movement as he/she moves the mic backwards and forwards, as inexperience can be clearly visible as well as audible (not forgetting that you may also have to consider that all-important logo).

And the rest ...

Covering more than two people becomes problematic without assistance, unless you're happy with the reporter and stick mic scenario. Your choice then lies between the stick mic on one channel and the camera mic on the other, or a radio/clip mic on the reporter and the stick mic to cover all other contributors. Circumstances and experience are your only guide to the best solution.

This, of course, assumes that the people are speaking. If they are under-taking some other form of noise generating activity, working with machinery, playing musical instruments and/or singing, then luck plays as great a part as judgement. If you can rehearse their activity, you can judge where best to place your mic, as well as how likely they are to faithfully repeat their performance. But if you have no control over events, you're almost certainly going to have to use the camera mic, and possibly position your reporter with another mic, and guide him/her into a suitable position for optimum sound pick-up (but see Section 2, Sound measurement; Phase, and Moving mics).

Stand mic

'I haven't got a mic stand in my kit!' I hear you cry. Well, I always carry a folding lightweight table stand (Figure 17.2(a),(b)) for its versatility in an emergency. As well as putting it on a flat surface, it can be gaffered to all sorts of other stands (Figure 17.3), equipment, bits of furniture, etc. To help with acoustic isolation, place a piece of thick foam/sponge rubber under its base, as they're particularly

(a)

(b)

Figure 17.2   (a) Folding table stand; (b) easily opens out to hold mic

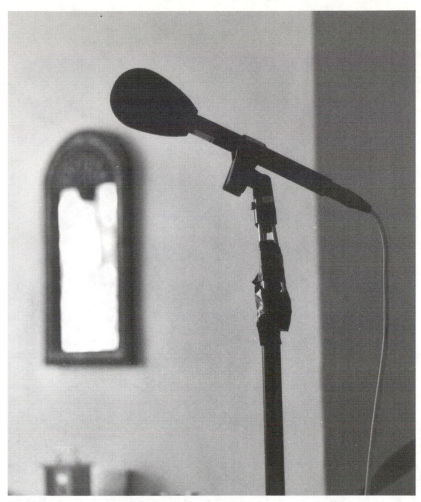

Figure 17.3 Table stand gaffered to lighting stand

prone to picking up noise transmitted via the table/desk top. You'll probably need to gaffer stand to rubber and rubber to table to secure it in position (but beware marking/damaging polished surfaces!), unless it is also going to appear in shot, in which case you must strive to make it as neat and unobtrusive as possible.

If you carry lighting stands, you should use the ones that have a screw thread (Figure 17.4(a),(b)) on the spigot in order that they can double as a mic stand in an emergency. But, although this may get you out of the odd tight spot, they don't have acoustically isolated bases and can all too easily pick up sound transmitted through the floor. Do not rely on them for anything

Figure 17.4 (a) Lighting stand with screw thread on spigot

Figure 17.4 (b) Screw thread on spigot in detail

other than desperation, although foam rubber placed under the feet will help, but if you do this, ensure that the stand remains stable.

Professional microphone stands come in all shapes and sizes, and are sturdy, thus relatively heavy, to ensure stability and improve acoustic isolation, together with rubber feet (Figure 17.5). My first choice is a gallows stand, with an arm to hold the microphone, an extremely flexible stand, which normally enables you to have both stand and microphone out of shot (Figure 17.6).

Whatever you use, it takes up space, and cramped conditions pose a problem. You need to place the mic in the correct position, but out of shot! A table stand is sometimes acceptable in shot (without the rubber, etc. underneath), which may prove one way of overcoming the problem. If you have pressed a lighting stand into use, you also have to position it such that it doesn't get knocked by being placed too close to your contributors (which is no doubt exactly where you need it for acceptable sound pick-up).

Care: whatever stand/mounting you use, always ensure that the cable is safely routed back to the camcorder, and gaffer it in place if necessary. Please also refer to Section 28, Sound recordist operation: multiple contributors; Mic stands, which has a more comprehensive overview of mounting mics and using stands at height.

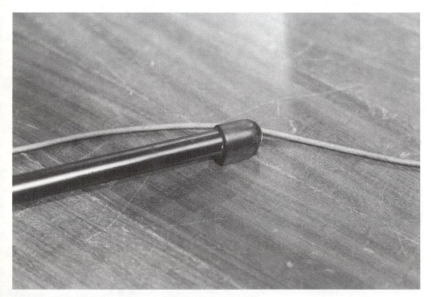

Figure 17.5   Rubber feet on mic stand

Figure 17.6 Gun mic on gallows stand

18 Single person operation: specific location scenarios

Walking and talking

Once your reporter is on the move, there's little choice other than a radio mic to avoid cable hazards. Assuming it's a clip mic, when he/she walks around, you have no control over its relationship to other sound sources, since it's in a fixed position, clipped to their clothing. So, if, for example, they move close to work-men using power tools or pneumatic drills, you cannot adjust the balance of their speech relative to the background noise.

This will almost certainly prove intolerable unless the source of the noise is *in vision*, which at least helps to explain its aural presence. But *you* will still be unable to adjust the balance between voice level and noise. However, it's a human trait to RAISE YOUR VOICE when trying to make yourself heard over a very loud noise. A professional reporter will invariably do this, which goes some way to overcoming the problem for you.

In these circumstances, you'll need to adjust the overall channel level which, if the camcorder is on your shoulder, will be on the front of the body/viewfinder. However, if the camcorder is on a tripod, you have the choice between the front control or the main channel gain on the recorder (see also Section 5, Camcorder: sound levels). The choice is purely personal, and depends in the main as to which is least likely to affect the shot, i.e. can you adjust the control without wobbling the camera?

With luck, that should provide you with acceptable sound, but the inexper-ienced/shy/nervous reporter may not automatically raise their voice. If this is the case, even riding the level control will almost certainly prove insufficient, and a retake is your only solution. Attempt to re-position the reporter to increase their distance from the source of the problem. Better still, try and persuade them that the piece works better in a static position, as far away from the noise as possible!

Press conference

A well-organized press conference is relatively easy to cover. A line feed from the PA will be available, although you'll probably need to supply your own XLR cable to plug it into your camcorder. (Beware the semi-pro system with an unbalanced output feed, a direct inject box may be necessary, see Section 9, Mics: cables and radio.) You can then either switch the camera mic to the second track, or put a radio mic on your reporter, if they are likely to ask questions at the Q&A.

However, if it's not been well-organized, you may wish to put a radio mic (on a table stand?) on the top table. If you do, you'll need to find out in advance who's going to speak in order to reassure yourself that it's correctly placed; and, from bitter experience, I can tell you that the organizers of these events often get that information wrong!

If there's PA, but no feed supplied (or it's unbalanced and you don't carry a DI box), either place your radio mic in front of a PA loudspeaker, or point your gun mic at one. Check the quality of the sound it produces beforehand, if at all possible, as they can be very variable. You may subsequently find you have to re-position your mic in front of another loudspeaker for acceptable results (it's always best to ascertain how many loudspeakers there are, together with their positions relative to your own operational area).

The worst case scenario is arriving late, after the proceedings have started, only to find that you're left with a poor camera position at the rear of the room, and then having to point a gun mic at the top table from this position as there's no PA. Intrepid operators may gallop up to the top table, bent over double to stay out of shot, and place a radio mic thereupon, but in an overcrowded room, don't count on it!

Phone conversation

Recording a phone conversation will depend on whether or not the phone handset has to be in vision, and whether the call is an 'actual' call in real-time, i.e. not staged. For an actual call, if the phone handset is in vision, you will need to conceal the mic and cable, and position the camera to ensure that they remain unseen. Using clear tape, stick the smallest clip mic you have close to the handset's earpiece (Figure 18.1), and secure the cable along the side of the handset away from the camera. Concealing it alongside and/or down the phone cable is problematic if the phone lead is both curly, and of a different colour to your mic cable (Figure 18.2). Providing you don't stretch the phone lead too much on shot, you should be able to get away with the mic lead down the centre of the curly lead. You could also try to ensure that shot-wise the backing behind the phone lead is dark enough to obscure the fact that there's a thinner one inside it!

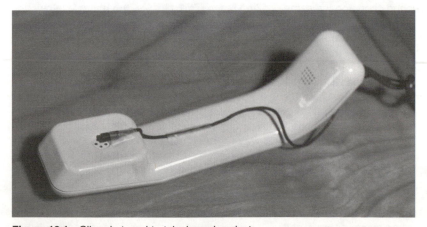

Figure 18.1 Clip mic taped to telephone handset

Figure 18.2 The mic lead is threaded inside the curly phone lead

Having taped the mic to the earpiece to pick up the incoming audio, you must advise your in-vision reporter not to move their head against the handset/mic capsule combination, in order to avoid unwanted rustling. Shoot the main conversation as wide as possible (depending on production requirements), using a second mic (gun?) for the reporter. Then shoot closer listening shots of them on the phone afterwards from a different angle, with the clip mic removed. You may also wish them to repeat some of the dialogue at the same time.

Depending on the facilities at your location, rather than attaching a mic to the earpiece of the phone that the reporter is holding, you could make use of a second phone on the same line and place a mic close to the handset. However, you must ensure that it is located some distance from your reporter in order to avoid interference. It is also advantageous to surround it with sound-deadening material, if you carry any (or use an on-site cushion or two). This is the preferred option as it does at least make for a visually neater result.

There are devices available 'over the counter' in some hi-fi/electrical stores which connect between the wall socket and phone, and produce an audio feed from the incoming phone signal. However, many modern switchboard systems employ digital signals, so this type of device would then only feed you 'digits'.

There is a fully professional way to record telephone conversations using a telephone balance unit (TBU), but you obviously need to know beforehand (and agree the extra cost of hiring the unit with production). The TBU keeps the line open and has a mic feed, but you need to send a feed of incoming audio to your reporter. This may necessitate the reporter wearing an earpiece with the audio feed, and holding the phone receiver up to their ear to cover it. This set-up may appear overly complicated, but should produce the best (and most reliable) sound from a phone. One point to note, however, it is preferable to originate the call from your end via the TBU, as you don't want it to ring when you're listening (ringing voltage on your input – ouch!).

It is important to understand that for the call to be used/broadcast, the person to whom you are speaking on the other end of the line must be aware that it is being recorded. If they do not, then their *privacy* must be observed, since an incoming call should not be recorded without them being fully aware of your actions. It is the production team's responsibility to obtain permission to broadcast contributions from any person or source (see also Section 15, Recording for the edit; Copyright) and they normally have to obtain a signed release form to this effect from all participants.

You'll probably gather from all of the foregoing that it is much simpler to stage the conversation, often using a call made by someone in an adjoining room. If you can (and you know that it can be accommodated in post-production) record both ends of the conversation clean, and let the phone frequency distortion be carried out in post-production. This reliably ensures the intelligibility of both ends of the conversation. In a real call, you may have interference on the line/circuit which necessitates a retake. Do not use mobile phones; the interference their operation generates is virtually impossible to overcome. If the call is supposed to be on a mobile (as an in-vision production requirement) it is best to stage it with clean sound as described.

Wind noise

We mentioned wind noise in the first section, and it can severely affect mic choice and placement. The most effective wind gag is the 'Dougal' (Figure 18.3), nick-named after the character in the children's serial 'The Magic Roundabout'. But it needs a reasonable surface area of 'hair' around the mic to work efficiently, and so doesn't lend itself to clip mics. It also needs regular grooming, a matted Dougal barely functions. Although a brush is supplied with each from new, better results may be obtained by using a small wire dog brush, available from pet shops.

If you're forced into using personal mics in windy situations, you'll have to protect them under clothing (assuming the sound is still intelligible) and/or use the reporter's body to mask them from the wind. This may compromise the shot, but in this instance the sound is almost certainly the more important element.

If wet, in the pavilion

Rain is another unwelcome element in location recording. Whilst your first thought may be to put up an umbrella, you'll find that the noise of the rain on the fabric is every bit as disconcerting as the sight of a rain swept reporter attempting a PTC. If you can re-position undercover, then that's the ideal solution.

If the rain shows no sign of stopping, and you're out in the middle of nowhere, and the piece has to be recorded at all costs ... you need a Plan B. The condenser mics are almost certainly going to complain if they get wet,

Figure 18.3 Gun mic in wind gag – 'Dougal'

with hisses, crackles and splats, not dissimilar to certain breakfast cereals. A dynamic mic should save the day, and would certainly be my first choice. However, a clip mic may well prove effective if you can protect it with a condom, making sure you keep the inside dry whilst rigging, of course; but I think you'll also have to make sure it's concealed or out of shot!

On-camera mic

The camera is very rarely the most suitable place to mount/position a mic, except for GVs (Figure 18.4). In this instance, it's frequently pointing in the correct direction, i.e. the way the camera's looking, although it's prone to camera handling noise, especially when operating the zoom control on the lens. However, if you're only using one other mic, switch the camera mic to track two, see also Section 20, Single person operation: tracks, levels and practical exercise (c); Which track?

Figure 18.4 On-camera mic

19   Single person operation: use of headphones

The only way you can tell exactly what you are recording, and the quality thereof, is by wearing headphones. If you're not constantly monitoring the sound track, it's all too easy to miss any fizz, crackle, pop or extraneous noise or interference which always manages to materialize at critical moments.

Choosing the correct headphones for everyday use is most important, as you need to ensure that they are of sufficient quality to accurately monitor your sound balance. At the same time, they should allow you to hear sound from around you, and be comfortable to wear for long periods of time. (See also Section 36, Equipment.)

Thus, having to use hired or pool equipment can be problematic with respect to consistent sound recording quality. I would suggest that if you are regularly sound recording as a freelance, you invest in your own pair of headphones, even if all other equipment is hired (or if you are an employee, persuade your employer of the value of these as a personal item) and always carry disinfectant wipes for cleaning purposes irrespective of whose headphones you are likely to use.

Another point to bear in mind, when operating the camera, you'll probably only be listening to one half of the headphones, as it's difficult to get your head fully in the viewfinder wearing full-sized headphones (see Headphone volume control, below).

In the same way that the viewfinder is your guide/monitor to the pictures you produce, your headphones are your guide/monitor to the sound you record. Any faults or imperfections with them will eventually show up in your end product. Nothing but experience can be your guide to judging whether noises heard during recording adversely affect your sound to the point at which you need to retake.

Your mics are in one position whilst your ears, and headphones, are in another. Telephones ringing, to take one obvious example, can often seem more intrusive to the producer and participants than they do on the sound track via the mics. At least you have the opportunity to replay any suspect parts of the recording to ascertain sound quality. My advice is to do this as often as possible, and to always check the last ten seconds of each take as a minimum.

Confidence replay
If, for any reason, you are unable to monitor whilst recording, the only way to guarantee that your soundtrack is free from faults is to replay and listen care-fully to the whole tape.

Headphone volume control
Since headphones come in a variety of impedances, feeding them via a volume control is essential to establish a comfortable and practical listening level (as

noted in Section 7, Camcorder: external facilities). Your listening level should be such that no sound leakage occurs which could upset or distract the contributors. This is even more important to bear in mind if you are operating with 'one ear on and one ear off' in respect of your headphones. If you work solely as a single person operator, you may find it useful to obtain a single-sided headset (Figure 19.1) for your convenience and comfort, in addition to your regular set of cans.

The volume control on the camera/recorder (often with the 'alarm' volume control beside it) rarely has any protection from accidental knocks or tweaks, so you MUST check its position regularly. Set it at the beginning of the day (before you go on location) so that you're monitoring your sound at a pre-determined level, and make a note of its position. Since you're reliant on your headphones to monitor sound levels, you must be vigilant that this control is not altered.

However, you may need to alter this level if you find yourself working in an exceptionally noisy environment. In order to hear anything at all, you may have to turn the volume up to its maximum, and even then you may experience difficulty in accurately monitoring your sound level and quality. Should you be faced with these conditions, always replay the tape in a quieter environment as soon as you can, to ensure that there were no unexpected problems, and return your headphone volume control to its original position. Take care not to work in overly noisy environments for long periods of time (see Section 16, Safety).

Figure 19.1 Single-sided headset makes looking into the viewfinder easier for single person operation

Also be aware that some headphones have a volume control in their cable (usually close to the split to each ear). If there is one there, turn it fully up, and gaffer tape it in that position.

Emergency spare

Carry at least one spare pair of lightweight headphones or earphones for use in emergencies (they only cost a few pounds, Figure 19.2). The mini-jack plugs on any headphones are their weakest link, and are prone to breakage.

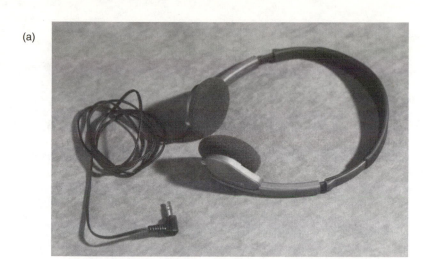

(a)

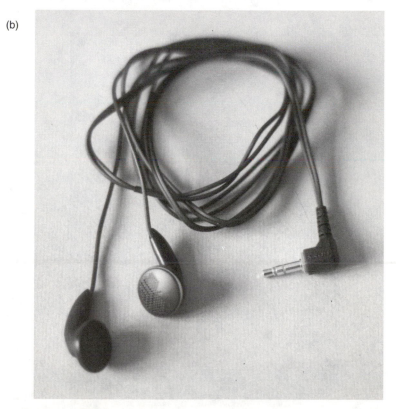

(b)

Figure 19.2 (a) Lightweight emergency spare headphones;
(b) emergency spare earphones

20 Single person operation: tracks, levels and practical exercise (c)

Which track?

Convention dictates that the main sound (i.e. your interviewee or reporter's PTC) goes on track one, and ancillary sound, (reporter's questions, or camera mic) on track two.

Since there are two tracks available, *always* record sound on both tracks, even if you are only using one mic. The general rule is, assuming you have one mic plugged to the camcorder on channel one, select the camera mic to channel two (Figure 20.1). In this way, should there be a problem with your main mic, you have an 'emergency' spare soundtrack, although almost certainly not of as good a quality.

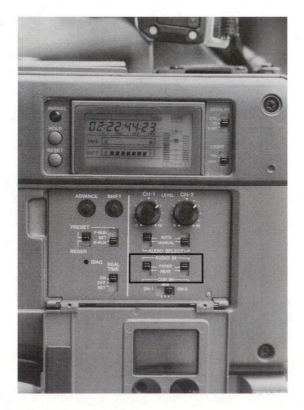

Figure 20.1   Select mics to each channel

Sound level

You won't be able to operate the camera and watch the meter/s simultaneously (see also Section 6, Camcorder: sound metering). There is usually an indication in the viewfinder showing incoming sound, but it's rarely sufficiently accurate to indicate the correct level. It does at least confirm that some audio is being recorded. Thus, we must rely on being able to hear with sufficient clarity via our headphones the accuracy of the sound levels during recording.

Practical exercise (c): pre-location

With everything plugged as you expect to use it on location, get your reporter/partner/friend/anyone who can speak, to keep talking whilst you turn the channel gain control fully up and down, monitoring on headphones. You must ensure that you have EE selected as your headphone feed, if there is a choice between PB or EE, as the PB selection may provide you with a falsely high reading (see Section 7, Camcorder: external facilities; Playback or E to E).

You'll soon hear the distortion that occurs at too high a level, and whilst watching your meter, you should reduce this until the voice level sounds correct, and the meter peaks at the values suggested (Section 6, Camcorder: sound metering). Repeat the gain adjustment fully up and down, and judge the correct level solely by listening, before looking at the meter for confirmation. Record at least thirty seconds of sound at the correct level, and replay it to check whether the replay level matches your input level.

You should repeat this practical several times, with each of your mics, and with the headphones covering only one ear – your left ear, assuming you're using your right eye to look in the viewfinder – the normal operating position. In this way, you will become familiar with how each mic sounds and also be able to judge the desired level solely by listening on headphones via one ear (see also Section 7, Camcorder: external facilities; Headphone volume control).

Gain

In Sections 10 and 11 (Mics: placement with regard to speech, and use of clip mic for seated interview) we noted the necessity of adjusting gain to cope with subject movement. This is a problem if you are feeding mics into the rear of a camcorder, since it's rarely practical to adjust levels via the individual channel gains on the recorder section, especially whilst it's hand-held/shoulder mounted. This only leaves the option of utilizing the channel one gain control mounted on the front of the viewfinder or camera body.

If you do decide to use this, start with it turned slightly down. Most are marked with a scale reading 0 to 10, in which case start your recording at about 7, or just over (Figure 20.2). This gives you a bit of an increase in hand if your contributors become too quiet, but plenty to decrease if they become louder (more frequently the case). Remember to increase the main channel one gain on the recorder section to compensate before you start, if this is not your normal mode of operation.

Only experience can tell you when you've achieved the correct level, and as well as avoiding distortion due to too high a level, be aware that too low a level

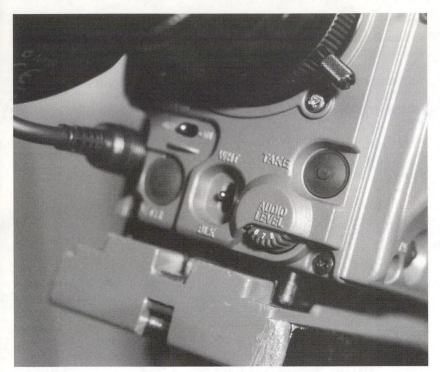

Figure 20.2 For single person operation, when using the channel one gain control on the camcorder body, start at around '7' on its scale, (with suitable compensation on the main channel gain control)

will be difficult to adequately correct later. Although it's possible to add some gain in post production, low level sound will be overcome by background hiss when this gain is added. Hence the need to undertake some form of practical exercise/s as outlined above, before venturing on location (especially with untried/hired equipment).

Camera mic selected to channel 2

Hand mic selected/plugged into channel 1

Figure 20.3 Reporter's piece to camera. Always use both sound tracks

21 Single person operation: shooting

On your shoot day, and before you leave home, you should consider if you, yourself, present the correct 'image' to your client and the contributors with whom you are working. 'Cleanliness is next to Godliness' is what I was told as a young lad, and I suggest you bear in mind that you may often be working in close proximity to a variety of people from all walks of life, probably for long periods at a time, some of whom may well be responsible for ensuring your continued employment. Your attire, freshly scrubbed appearance and demeanour all count to the good, if not more so than being able to competently handle the equipment.

So, having looked in the mirror, the next thing to do is to carefully check the details from the call sheet to satisfy yourself that you have all the required equipment stowed and ready to go. You should always check each item of equipment to ensure it's operating satisfactorily before you leave your base. (See Section 34, Pre-location equipment check.)

At the location

Meet production at the R/V as specified on the call sheet (see Section 38, Call sheet details). If you were unable to speak to them beforehand, spend the first few minutes discussing the shoot. They should:

- Outline the finished product.
- Indicate whether there has been a previous shoot, if shots needs matching, and if there is to be any future shooting for the same item.
- Specify the order of interviewees and whether they should be facing right to left, or left to right, where applicable.
- Provide details of shots/effects/problems specific to location.
- Clearly indicate any hazards/risks following the location assessment if they are not included on the call sheet, and identify other possible problems, e.g. interviewee availability, parking restrictions, site access, etc. has enough time been allowed, is there any slack?
- Contingency plans, or where things may differ from plan.

Discussion beforehand minimizes any risks posed by potential problems which may disrupt the shoot.

Line-up

You should *always* record a minimum of thirty seconds line-up (colour bars in vision, and camera mic selected so that tone is recorded, if the camcorder provides this as a facility) at the beginning of each cassette, and preferably up to one minute if you can afford the time. This ensures that you aren't using the first part of the cassette which often doesn't have the tape correctly tensioned (which may be due to possible loosening whilst being shipped/transported). Even in a tearing hurry, always spool into the tape so that you don't use the first ten to fifteen seconds for any vital pictures/sound.

Shooting for the edit

Before you run to record, questions to ask are, will the soundtrack be used as a stand-alone piece, what comes before and after the piece, will it be edited, if so how, and at what length, and will any other sound/music be added/dubbed? As well as these considerations regarding the soundtrack, no shot stands alone, and most of the time you'll be concentrating on shooting a series or sequence of shots, with a view to how they'll be cut together, and providing the editor with as wide a choice as possible.

To achieve this end, if you're like me, you'll be mentally judging the edit points as you're shooting. But whilst managing sound and pictures together in this way, you'll soon notice that good edit points are rarely achieved in both at the same point. In an interview, the cut point is more often than not governed by the answers, i.e. the sound, so you must be aware of the consistency of sound level relative to the background/ambient noise. In other words, if a particularly noisy motorbike goes roaring past the window during an interview, the poor editor will find it impossible to disguise an edit within that time frame without the assistance of some covering sound from another source (see Section 15, Recording for the edit; Wildtrack). The ear is particularly sensitive to changes in both quality and level, so even a quietly ticking clock in the background will prove an impossible edit to conceal if a single tick is displaced in time!

However, in a sequence of someone physically performing a task for example, the edit is almost always visually led. But with their every movement, some sound will be generated, so it must be in sync, and if a cutaway is added in the edit, there must be sufficient relevant sound track to cover it. In many cases, the sound taken during the cutaway may not be used, but you should always record sound when shooting in spite of assurances that 'It won't be needed'. In fact, a Golden Rule to observe is:

■ Never shoot mute pictures.

Always ensure that you at least have the camera mic selected (preferably to both tracks), as this will then provide the editor with a guide track of what's happening on location. Another advantage of this is that you can also add verbal notes relating to the shoot and the shot/s, a real bonus in post-production, believe me.

'Did you get that?'

At minimum, *always* confidence check the last ten seconds of your first shot on location, and the final ten seconds of each recorded cassette. It is good working practice to develop the habit of checking the final few seconds of recorded material at each and every recording break.

Whilst recording, if you suspect a problem you should avoid stopping someone in 'full flow' if at all possible. Faults and/or warning lights may intrude during an interview, and if it's simply a case of an imminent tape or battery change, then you should let the contributor finish their answer before stopping. The fine point of judgement you have to make is when the fault is such that further recording becomes impossible until it has been rectified. Do you wait for the end of an answer, or butt in (with an apology) and notify production of the problem? Only experience can be your guide in this situation, but as a general rule, working with experienced contributors, it's unlikely that they'll be unduly upset if you interrupt. However, with inexperienced or nervous contributors, it's probably better to wait, if you're unlikely to lose more than a minute by doing so. More than that, and everyone's time is being wasted.

Cassette handling

- Keep them *clean*. Dirt and dust will cause head clog and wear.
- *Label* each cassette with the date, title, and a rough indication of content, plus any technical details that may assist the edit (e.g. interviewee on track 1).
- When you remove the cassette from the recorder, *immediately* push in/slide the red indicator to prevent over-recording (record inhibit).
- Do not re-use cassettes, they may suffer from tape distortion through previous maltreatment, or contain dirt or dust, or have a damaged oxide layer through over-use, all of which leads to drop-out and replay malfunction.
- *Never* let your cassettes come into contact with, or be stored/carried close to mobile phones.

At the end of the day/shoot, *ensure that all tapes/rushes* are handed to production or safely despatched/delivered to a pre-arranged address.

Transcription recording

You may be asked to provide a transcription recording on a cassette recorder. Many reporters carry their own, and often find that its onboard mic provides sufficient quality for their purposes. Some camcorders provide outputs from channels one and two, which you could use to feed a cassette recorder, always providing you have the correct plugs/leads to interface with the one they produce. You may wish to carry one of your own, with reliable connections, but most people would consider this too much to ask of single person operation. See also Section 26, Sound recordist operation: balancing; Transcription recording.

Sync

When single camera video recording first began, the idea that you might have to use a clapper board for sync would have been considered ludicrous. These days, however, with digital processing and compression being applied to pictures, there's a distinct possibility that the sound can end up out of sync at a later date. You will be thanked by many an editor if you simply record an in-vision hand-clap on each of your takes. Better still, if you've time to write it up, use a clapper board to identify each take visually, together with its distinctive sound.

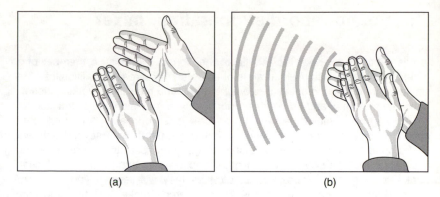

(a)   (b)

Figure 21.1   At the beginning of every take, record a hand clap in frame to provide a
sound and vision sync point

22 Sound recordist operation: mixer

In this section, you wear the mantle of the Sound Recordist, a member of a professional team, with a wider range of equipment and responsibilities than the single operator. You're solely responsible for sound recording, working closely with a cameraman, and on larger productions you may also be responsible for supervising other members of a sound crew. As you become more experienced, you will be expected to work together with staff from several different backgrounds and disciplines. You should always respect the experience and knowledge that your colleagues in other departments bring to the production (make-up, costume, props, sparks, etc.) as they will respect you and your views. Before you reach this stage in your career, make sure that you take the time to understand every person's role in the programme making chain, and how all of you interact with each other in order to work together as a team, *no one discipline is more important than another*.

Operationally, you're now using mics fed via a mixer to the camcorder, monitoring on headphones, and feeding both tracks of the recorder. Nevertheless, at this juncture we'll only consider mono recording, and tackle stereo separately (see Sections 29 and 30). This section builds on the information from previous sections, rather than repeat everything about camcorder audio facilities, mic placement, shooting for the edit, etc. In order to avoid confusion, in the sections which are prefixed as 'Sound Recordist Operation', 'channel' refers to mixer facilities and 'track' refers to recorder facilities.

Portable location mixer
The vast majority in use today are four channel capable, enabling you to mix up to four separate sources (Figure 22.1). For the majority of location work, they are operated whilst slung around the recordist's neck via a strap, and experience is needed to adjust them to find a comfortable position in which to 'wear' one all day (Figure 22.2). They are often contained within a weatherproof pouch, which can hold extra items of equipment, for example, spare batteries, screwdriver, radio mic with transmitter/receiver, etc. This being so, ensure that your mixer/pouch combination has a reasonably wide and padded strap to spread the load on your shoulder/s. The mixer itself provides a range of facilities, but you *must refer to the handbook* in order to confirm whether the one you are using has all the features listed below.

(a) Channel inputs
Each channel is switchable between mic and line level inputs, and normally has additional switched attenuation, most commonly 10 dB and 20 dB, and/or a coarse gain control in order to give each fader precision control within a wide range. There is also switched provision for phantom or T-powered mics. Switchable bass cut is available usually in two steps, commonly 4 dB and 10 dB, at 50 Hz and/or 100 Hz, or at 75 Hz and 150 Hz (Figure 22.3).

Figure 22.1   SQN4 portable location mixer in pouch

On location, plug the inputs in a logical fashion. For instance, from your operating position you could have the contributors, as seen from left to right, plugged from channels one to four. Or you may prefer to stick to a personal working set-up, for example: channels one and two – clip and/or radio mics; channel three – stick mic; and channel four – gun mic; or for press conferences, gun on three and PA on four. Your working preferences will probably be dictated by the layout and 'feel' of the faders on whichever mixer you're using.

On a stereo capable mixer there will be pan pots for each channel, and a channel gang switch for at least channels one and two, if not three and four as well, and the facility to gang limiters (see Section 30, Stereo: mixer).

(b) Outputs

There are at least two pairs of balanced outputs, main (multi-pin) and auxiliary (3-pin XLRs), each may also have a gain control sited at the side of the mixer, although the outputs are fed primarily via the main gain control. There is also an unbalanced output, suitable for feeding a separate recorder, e.g. DAT or transcription (Figure 22.4).

The overall amount of compression and limiting may be variable/switchable. A compressor circuit acts in a similar fashion to a knee circuit in the video signal, and proportionally reduces the level when it rises above a pre-determined point (the onset or threshold). This onset may be variable/switchable as may the proportion of compression applied to the signal (2:1, 3:1, etc.). A limiter is a compressor with a high ratio, at least 18:1, with the onset close to peak. Thus, any momentary high-level signal, a gunshot for example, which would distort when passed without limiting, is held when its level reaches the pre-

Figure 22.2 Sound recordist using a mixer harness over both shoulders – good load-spreading

Figure 22.3 Mixer input panel

determined threshold. The limiter decay time may also be variable, and for optimum use is set to around 0.1 to 0.2 second.

(c) Powering

Most models run on a nominal 12 V supply, often 8 AA dry cells loaded internally, but the operational voltage range may be approximately 9–14 V. There is a power switch which either offers internal or external powering in addition to 'off',

Figure 22.4 Mixer output panel

or the mixer may detect when power is available on its external feed, and switch from the dry cells to external automatically. The external power socket will accept 12 V from a rechargeable battery via a suitable lead, the slim NP1 being a popular choice with recordists. (If the mixer runs on AA cells, you'll probably find that rechargeable AA cells do not provide sufficient voltage to run it for any length of time, if at all, as their nominal maximum is 1.2 V per cell as opposed to the 1.5 V per dry cell.)

The mixer dies when power drops below approximately 9 V, and most mixers have a battery check facility (often via one of the meters). A safety feature of most mixers is that the audio monitoring facility loses signal (in other words, your headphones begin to 'die') before the mixer output, so you can tell if and when batteries need replacing during a lengthy recording prior to any deleterious effect to the main sound output.

(d) Metering and monitoring

Most stereo capable mixers intended for broadcast use have two PPMs for metering. They may follow mixer signal output only, or switch metering to follow the headphone monitoring selection. The headphone monitoring will normally be via either a standard quarter inch (6 mm) jack or mini 3.5 mm jack socket, with an associated volume control. You must set your headphone monitoring level before you start any other work, and note the position of the volume control. Since the mixer is unlikely to leave your hands, it is extremely unlikely that this control will be accidentally altered, but it always pays to be careful.

Headphone monitoring includes most, if not all, of the following: mixer output, return feed from camcorder, A/B stereo, A or B in both ears, M/S stereo, M or S, each channel independently, PFL – pre-fade listen, which allows you to monitor the input to a channel before opening the fader. (See also Section 24, Sound recordist operation: mixing mics; PFL.)

(e) Tone

The mixer may provide a selection of 'standard' tones for test/line-up purposes (see also Section 6, Camcorder: sound metering; Meter summary), and certainly mono and stereo tone. Stereo tone idents at least one channel (usually the left).

Mixer/recorder

There are currently mixers available incorporating an onboard hard disc recorder. This facility is slowly making inroads into productions which previously used separate Nagra and DAT recorders. They do, however, use more power than a stand-alone mixer, and are heavier. If you use 12 V rechargeable batteries for power, and have a couple of radio mics and transmitters/receivers in the mixer pouch, alongside spare dry cells, XLR sex-change barrels, phase reverse lead, and a tweaker or two, then slinging the whole lot round your neck for a day's work may not be entirely practical. (I never cease to be amazed at the detritus carried in the average sound recordist's mixer pouch, kangaroos have nothing on them!)

The other advantage to using this facility is that you no longer need the umbilical cable between your mixer and the camcorder, although do ensure you select the camera mic (preferably to both recorder tracks) to at least provide a guide track, in the event you decide to dispense with a cable feed altogether. You almost certainly *do* need a feed of timecode from the camcorder to your recorder. (A word of caution with respect to timecode – to date, the majority of camcorders do not possess sufficiently accurate onboard timecode generators to ensure they run in sync with other equipment unless a locking feed is provided, or they themselves are the master, see also Section 33, Timecode.) The feed can be cabled, but that defeats one of the advantages of this set-up. There are radio timecode systems available, but problems in the signal path can render gaps in the timecode, and thus throw up horrendous problems in post production. The best solution is to use accurately set timecode generators, such as Lockit boxes (Figure 22.5), feeding each item of equipment.

Figure 22.5 Lockit box mounted on the side of a camcorder (courtesy Ambient Recording GmbH)

23 Sound recordist operation: track selection

Camcorder plugging

There are many differing cables and connectors available to couple the mixer to the camcorder. Broadcast camcorders have XLR inputs, and the simplest method of connecting the two is to run two XLR cables from the mixer, to feed tracks one and two. More often than not, though, in the field of broadcasting most sound recordists will use one of the more specialist cables and connectors which consists of a single outer housing with several cables contained therein. As well as sending sound to the camcorder these 'multi-core' cables provide the facility to receive a combination of return information including audio monitoring, cueing, video, timecode, and even power from the camera battery.

On the other hand, should your work involve smaller DV equipment, you may find that you have an option to purchase specialized interface boxes/connectors which can either be off-the-shelf, or even made to order, in the event that you are not yet fully confident to wield a smouldering soldering iron. In this field, though, there are too many variations (and continuing developments) to present any form of comprehensive list herein.

Whilst having all the information provided by a multi-cable connection is often useful, in the broadcast arena these cables are heavier, and more expensive than a simple pair of XLRs. Your cameraman may not thank you for adding to his/her load! If a fault occurs, unless you carry a spare (expense!) it's a good idea to have several XLRs to fall back on.

However, since speed is so often of the essence, the majority of recordists opt for the single multi-core cable between the camcorder and themselves, in spite of the extra expense and slight additional weight. Always beware: the problem with using more than one lead/cable is that two or more can all too easily tangle together, and cause problems when fast coupling/uncoupling is required. Should you opt for the two XLRs route to feed the camcorder, I suggest that you ensure that they're both the same length, and that you tape them together at regular intervals along their length to avoid the mad spaghetti heap that can all-too-easily materialize under your nose, when least expected.

To further minimize the risk of this unseemly happenstance, whatever cable/s you use, do not leave more than is necessary between the camcorder and yourself. Coil any excess at your own end and attach it to the mixer in such a way that it can easily be loosened if the cameraman suddenly hares off after that vital shot (Figure 23.1). At the start of the working day, many recordists attach 'tails' to the camcorder (or some form of 'breakout box') allowing for that all important swift coupling/uncoupling (Figure 23.2).

Without re-hashing information from previous sections, with the mixer connected to the camcorder, make sure that you have selected line level input for each of the tracks. Moreover, unless you are feeding the same sound to each

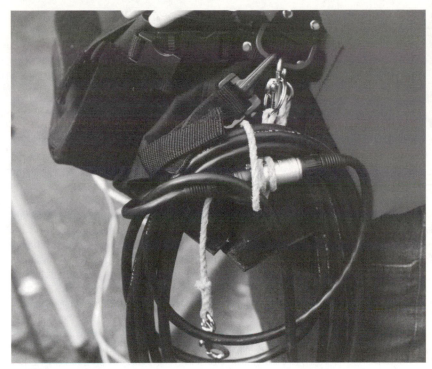

Figure 23.1 Cable coiled on mixer

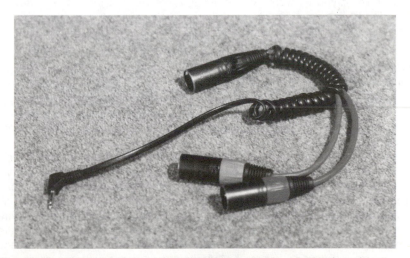

Figure 23.2 'Tails' used to attach mixer lead to camcorder, allowing for quick disconnection

track, check that you've correctly fed tracks one and two. For peace of mind, different coloured glands or cables are a boon, since a swift glance at the plugged ends is all the reassurance you need to establish that everything is connected as it should be. When you do a line-up, check the last few seconds of recording to ascertain that all is working as expected, and that your track selection and levels are correct.

Working apart

There will be times when the cameraman you're working with will go off and shoot by him/herself, using the camera mic to provide a guide track. When the two of you 're-connect' it is *vital* to check that you've re-selected 'line' input to both recorder tracks, and that your mixer is correctly re-plugged. *Do not* rely on the cameraman doing this (and I speak as a cameraman myself!).

The cameraman may also rely on you selecting the camera mic in the first place, before he/she goes off in search of his/her illustrative shots. And it's usually best if you do so, since, as sound recordist, you're nominally in charge of all the audio recorded on location, even though you may not actually be plugged into the camcorder and monitoring the results at all times! In this event, for safety's sake you may opt to select manual level to track one, and auto level to track two, since this should cover just about any conceivable shooting scenario.

However, some cameramen/productions prefer to have the camera mic selected to track two at all times, regardless of whether your mixer is connected or not, which is more an ENG style of operation. They may even dictate whether they want it in auto or manual mode (meaning they will probably insist on 'auto' in spite of your protests). As a sound recordist, you may have to accept this, even though you would prefer to use both tracks for your mixer output when connected. If you do work like this though, ensure that track one is *always* switched to line level on the rear input, and that you write up the cassette box/label to this effect.

Radio link

An alternative to having a cable between the camcorder and the mixer is to radio link the sound feed between them. Some productions/cameramen may insist on this set-up, and whilst it can provide great flexibility of working and freedom of movement for both the camera and mic positioning, it has its share of pitfalls.

You will have to mount a radio receiver on the camcorder, which not only adds to its weight, but almost certainly also affects/alters the balance. This may prove problematic either when operating on the shoulder/hand-held or tripod mounted camcorder (depending on the range and flexibility of the panning head). The receiver needs to be powered, and this is best done via the camcorder battery if the facility exists, since in this configuration, any battery failure precludes the possibility of further shooting. I hope this is an obvious statement, but you must always be aware of when the camcorder is turning over, so that you're sending correctly balanced sound at this point in time.

Plus, just to keep you on your toes, there are several reasons why the mixer output may not be recorded, among them:

- Your transmitter develops a fault/battery dies.
- The receiver develops a fault/battery dies.
- RF problems/interference, as outlined in Section 9, Mics: cables and radio, Radio mic rules.
- The cameraman doesn't notice the lack of sound.

As with using radio mics, the only safe way to ensure that you have a complete sound track is to replay all of it at the end of a take. Should this prove impractical, or if you're covering an unrepeatable event, then, for peace of mind, and to allay heart failure, make a back-up recording. At minimum this should be on MiniDisk, if not DAT (or Nagra). Hopefully, as mixer/recorder combinations become more commonplace, these problems will be alleviated.

24 Sound recordist operation: mixing mics

Mics

It is impossible to provide a definitive list of mics that constitute a 'working' kit for a recordist. Much depends on the type of work you're engaged on, and/or the equipment provided by your employer. Nevertheless, as a bare minimum, I would expect a recordist to have one gun mic, one dynamic reporter's (stick) mic, two clip mics, and a radio clip mic (which may be provided instead of one of the line-fed clip mics).

Mic placement has been dealt with in previous sections (see Sections 10 and 11, Mics: placement with regard to speech, and Use of clip mic for seated interview; and Sections 17 and 18, Single person operation: mic placement overview and static operation, and Specific location scenarios), but a word to the wise, do remain open-minded when others offer suggestions. Experienced artists often have advice on how best to mic their performance, for example, I've known bassists and guitarists suggest how and where to put mics in/on their instruments, producing exactly the desired result. In the case of musicians, many have spent a lifetime striving to achieve a certain sound from their instruments, so do respect their comments.

Mixing

With four channels 'at your fingertips', it may seem that the best way to cover that number of contributors is to put a mic on each person and fade them all up at once. By all means try it and see, but each mic is essentially a source of noise, and for every fader you open you raise the 'base' level of ambient sound. The further each one is opened, the more 'noise' you add – definitely not to be recommended.

However, assuming that the circumstances you find at your location dictate that you have to mic each of your contributors individually, as outlined above, then before you start recording you need to establish a voice level for each person in turn (it's the 'What did you have for breakfast?' scenario all over again!). To do this, ask each person to speak one at a time, and open their channel fader to what you judge to be the correct level and make a note of its position (how it feels under your fingertips). Having established four fader positions, once you start recording, you have to keep all faders at as low a level as possible, apart from opening to your pre-determined level, the one for who-ever's speaking. Depending on their conversational level, you may have to slightly alter the amount to which you fade up each individual contributor.

Whilst listening to your output is therefore of the utmost importance, you also have to watch your contributors, and anticipate who's likely to speak (so you won't have much time to look at your meters or the faders themselves). Only open the channel fader of the person who's speaking, to around your pre-determined full voice level. You'll probably find that the ideal working position for the other three faders will be somewhere around less than half of their pre-determined speech level position. However, if one contributor is fidgeting, or making distracting noises, you may have to reduce their level even more. Ideally, none of the faders will be fully closed, but there are no hard and fast rules. If more than one person starts talking at once you instantly have an editorial decision to make, whose speech do you let dominate?

Well that depends on whether you (meaning the production) have control of the discussion, and can repeat any sections that prove unclear. That's certainly the safest option, a retake of any interrupted speech, so that you get each contributor to separate their comments. If the conversation is a 'once only' opportunity, then the safest option is almost certainly to let the camera be your guide. The viewer/listener can only see whoever is in shot, so you need to be in a position to see the direction in which the camera is pointing. You must be able to judge the size of the shot it's taking, and thus how many of the speakers are in vision.

Judging shot size

You'll probably find it helpful if you can see a video monitor, too, but do take the time to think about how the camera positions itself for each shot. On a single, the camera's lens will be pointing directly at the person (Figure 24.1), but on a wide shot, the camera lens will almost certainly be pointed at the middle of the group, and tilted down (Figure 24.2). Use any rehearsal time to study the shots and the camera positions so that you're aware of how the cameraman will react to unexpected comments. It may be that the director will already have arranged that, in the event of a free-for-all, he/she would like the shot to stay with one particular person. If this is so, although you may need to ensure that their sound

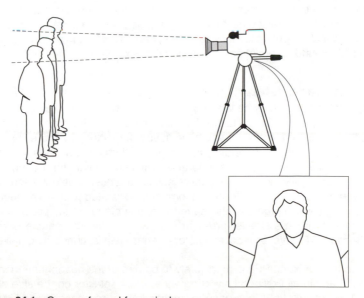

Figure 24.1 Camera framed for a single

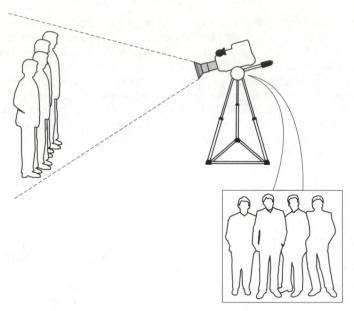

Figure 24.2 Camera framed for a WS

remains predominant, you'll still need to be able to hear questions and comments directed at them.

From the foregoing you can see that smoothly mixing between contributors takes experience, and can only be done by listening to your output, especially when voices become raised (and intermingled), as you will almost certainly have to judge most of the output level by ear alone, and adjust faders accordingly (see Section 25, Sound recordist operation: practical exercises (d) and (e)).

PFL – pre-fade listen

Pre-fade listen (which may be labelled 'pre-hear' on some sound desks) can be very reassuring to enable you to check an incoming sound feed, prior to actually fading it up. The more channels you have at your fingertips, the more important you'll find this facility, and certainly any large multi-channel mixer/sound desk (see Section 28, Sound recordist operation: multiple contributors) almost certainly has an easily accessible button associated/beside/below each fader which you can press to monitor the incoming feed related to that channel. On these desks, you will probably also have the option of monitoring via your main loudspeakers, or via a smaller pre-hear unit, which may also handle talkback (see Section 31, Live broadcasting, for further details concerning talkback facilities).

On portable mixers, PFL is more likely to be part of the headphone monitoring circuit, and in all likelihood switched via a rotary selector on the side of the mixer. This may make it less easy to access in a hurry, especially when the mixer is in a protective carrying case slung over your shoulder, but there are some instances when it can bail you out of an impending disaster.

You may remember that the advice given in Section 22, Sound recordist operation: mixer, was to plug your contributors to the input channels in a logical order. Herewith a cautionary tale! All goes smoothly until a break in recording (often to change a tape or battery), at which stage some or all of the participants also take a break, removing their mics themselves, and casually discarding them on their chairs. Once the tape/battery has been changed, the director is chivvying said participants to hurry back to their places, and insists that the cameraman runs to record immediately the 'bums are on the seats'. Although you were distracted when said participants sat down, and put their mics back on, looking up as the cameraman says 'At speed', you realize that in the rush to resume recording, the mics have been swapped around (and of course, all your clip mics look the same!). Fortunately PFL allows you to check who's wearing which one without necessarily stopping everything again (and upsetting the overwrought director).

A similar situation might arise if you are unable to see your participants (and although the sound recordist may get his/her own mixing area – with a chair! – due to the 'exigencies of the location' it may well be around a corner or behind a pillar) and again PFL comes to your rescue. In more straightforward operations, you may need it to monitor a radio mic, especially if you've been having trouble with that particular channel/frequency combination (see Section 9, Mics: cable and radio for more information on radio mics and their problems). In one instance, I can even recall two sports broadcasters who managed to swap their radio mics (complete with transmitters) during a break in the recording of an event we were covering, and the sound recordist only spotted the mistake (well, they claimed it was) when checking PFL.

However, you must bear in mind that when you are using PFL, you are monitoring the source *before* the relevant fader. Therefore the level of incoming sound is determined by the coarse gain setting for that channel, and *does not* correspond to the level as heard in your overall balance via the fader; in fact, you will almost certainly perceive it to be at a lower level. Hence, you *must not* make any balance or level decisions solely using PFL as a reference.

So, as a reminder:

- PFL should only be used to determine the presence of and identitfy a source.
- The level you hear does not relate to your overall balance.
- The use of PFL does not alter or affect your overall balance.

25 Sound recordist operation: practical exercises (d) and (e)

Practical exercise (d): mixing

To gain experience, and harking back to Section 13, Mics: practical listening exercise (b) – mic placement and sound discrimination, move the loudspeakers as far apart as possible, and feed the same sound to each. If you can select speech on your radio as the loudspeaker feed, that is the ideal for this exercise. Place a mic in front of each loudspeaker and plug them to convenient channels on your mixer. (If you're unable to select the same source to each loudspeaker, use a single loudspeaker with both mics pointing at it – and unplug the other. Although this should provide the same result, experience shows that the two loudspeaker system works better, always providing they both match, that is.)

Monitoring on headphones (just checking!), fade up one mic to provide you with a satisfactory level (let's say peaking 4 on the PPM). Now, gently cross-fade between your two mics – keeping the level exactly the same, so that you're unable to hear any rise or dip in the overall sound output level. Keep your eye on the meter, but with a varying level of sound source, such as speech, you'll find it nowhere near as exact a reference as your ear for maintaining the desired level.

If you have two further mics available, place one beside each of the other mics and plug them to your other two channels. Repeat the exercise, mixing between adjacent channels in order, 1, 2, 3, 4, and then alternate, 1, 3, 1, 4, 2, for example. Once you're satisfied that you can achieve a reasonably smooth result, record one complete sequence through all four channels. Your recording may be on a quality audio cassette or minidisk system, or on a camcorder (there is no point to listening to it via an inferior system, such as a transcription unit, as you may not be able to accurately judge the consistency of your efforts). The added advantage to utilizing a camcorder is that you can also familiarize yourself with its plugging, should this be necessary.

Before you play it back, let me ask you, what was the person you've just recorded talking about? Embarrassing, isn't it? Nine times out of ten the recordist is so concerned with listening to levels and sound quality, that he/she doesn't follow the content. That's the next skill you have to acquire, because if there's ever a production debate about 'What did he say?' the first person to be asked is the recordist.

When you do replay this exercise, you should do so on loudspeakers, so that you can assess the sound as a listener. Ask yourself, is there any noticeable difference between the sound quality you heard on headphones and the quality from the loudspeakers? Is there any discernable change in the level?

Practical exercise (e): mixing and balancing

This exercise works best if you can have someone read a lengthy passage from, say, a book or a newspaper. Place them well away from the two loudspeakers, and place a mic at a suitable distance in front of them to record their reading, and so that it does not noticeably pick up sound from the loudspeakers. Select a different source to each loudspeaker, preferably music, and place a mic in front of each one.

Fade up your reader, and slowly mix in sound from one loudspeaker 'beneath' the speech, until you have a suitable balance between speech and music. Now cross-fade the two music sources (the mics in front of the loudspeakers) to provide a smooth transition 'behind' the speech. Record your results (on a quality system, as before), cross-fading backwards and forwards between the two music sources every twenty seconds or so, for a couple of minutes.

Replay your results, and again ask yourself, does the balance between speech and music sound the same as it did on headphones? Is it the balance you were trying to achieve, the music not too loud or too quiet behind the voice? Are the transitions between the background music sections subtle enough for the listener to accept as 'natural' or 'believable'?

26 Sound recordist operation: balancing

The balancing act
Once you're satisfied with your mixing ability, you must ensure that you're able to operate without having to constantly look down at the mixer panel. Obviously, watching a discussion amongst contributors to anticipate the next speaker, you must know the operational position of your faders by touch alone. You must also recognize the sound level you require by listening to the output, so that you don't need to continuously watch the meters, an occasional glance is all that should be necessary.

Deliberate sound peak
However, meters are a guide to keeping the overall dynamic range of your output to within about 20 dB, the broadcast requirement. Although it gives you peace of mind to know you can rely on the limiter holding back sudden peaks, there are times when you want to give the listener the experience of a sudden jump in sound level. Thus, sound peaks must be anticipated, and levels adjusted to cope. From the listener's perspective, what matters is to retain the impression of a change in level, and so you may need to gently reduce the overall level preceding a peak, to preserve the desired effect. From this you will gather that *rehearsal* of critical items/material is to be recommended.

A further problem of wildly varying sound levels on location is that your ears can be fooled into believing that the level they're monitoring is correct, when the ambient level has altered so much that their sensitivity has been either lowered or heightened. Beware; this is the time to keep a close watch on the meters.

The perfect mix?
You've honed your skills to perfection, and your programme mix effortlessly glides from one contributor to another. But is a programme mix necessarily the ideal for post-production? 'I can't separate these sounds!' is the wail from the edit suite, following yet another change of mind from production.

You may have the capability of mixing several sources together, but don't lose sight of the end result. You still need to give the (dubbing) editor plenty of choice, especially in the face of ever-varying production requirements. Take one example, the one-to-one interview. For maximum flexibility, the post-production requirement is almost certainly each voice on a separate track.

Split track
Assuming you plug the inputs such that one person's mic is selected to channel one, and the other to channel two, then via the mixer, you can split track by feeding the left leg (channel one) panned hard left to track one, and the right leg (channel two) panned hard right to track two (obviously, check that you haven't ganged the faders). If production prefer, you could split track and offer answers (the interviewee) on track one, pan pot central (going to both tracks), and a programme mix of questions and answers (interviewer panned hard right) on

track two. The latter option does need a firm decision beforehand to ensure it's the ideal answer to a dubbing editor's dream.

Transcription recording

You may be asked to provide a transcription recording on a cassette recorder. This does not have to be broadcast quality as it is for use by the reporter, who can listen to it to select the pieces they require (often in the car on the way back from location) and/or by production staff at base in preparing a script to assist the edit. Many reporters carry one of their own, and often find that its onboard mic provides sufficient quality for their purposes. However, if they prefer a feed of your programme sound, you can send them one from the unbalanced output of the mixer, always providing you have the correct plugs/leads to interface with the equipment they produce. Make sure you check the input level is correctly set, and that it is recording satisfactorily before the interview. For peace of mind, carry one of your own with reliable connections and known recording characteristics.

Unless used regularly, it's the one piece of kit that causes most grief to sound recordists (apart from radio mics), since they frequently forget to start them. Dubbing a cassette of an important interview from the camcorder during a break in shooting can be extremely frustrating (and embarrassing!). If the interview is protracted, change the audio cassette every time you change the video cassette (make sure the audio cassettes are the correct length), as another embarrassing moment is when the cassette recorder goes 'CLICK' during the interview when its tape ends. This can also happen if the battery dies, so ensure that you put fresh ones in before recording, and carry plenty of spares. If you are shooting more than one interview for an item/programme, use a fresh cassette for each interview. When you remove cassettes from your recorder, *label each one clearly*, as the most embarrassing moment is when you discover you've just taped over a previous interview.

27 Sound recordist operation: pole operation

Working with a gun mic on a fish pole (Figure 27.1(a),(b)) is an extremely flexible method of operation, and often the quickest means of placing the mic in the desired position. However, as mentioned earlier, assistance is not always available/affordable as and when you like, so as well as operating the mixer, you'll have to be able to manoeuvre the pole at the same time. Depending on circumstances, you can either work with one hand on the mixer and the other

Figure 27.1 (a) Sound recordist holding the gun mic on a pole

Figure 27.1 (b) Gun mic on a pole

hand holding the pole with one end tucked under you arm, or wedged against your body; or you can hold the pole with both hands.

Using both hands is not as strange as you may think, and if you're operating on a windy exterior, with the pole at its full extension carrying a gun mic in its cradle and wind gag, then you'll need both hands to control it! Set an acceptable level on the mixer and vary the position of the mic to accommodate changes in level from your subject. Thus, if a person raises their voice, you have a choice of either using the channel fader on the mixer, or backing the mic off a few inches, depending on circumstances (and hands!). A combination of these two operations will help you maintain control over the relationship between the levels of speech and ambient sound.

However, with regard to ambient sound, be careful to keep the mic in the same plane when poling between contributors. This normally means keeping the mic vertical (Figure 27.2) and swinging the pole in a horizontal arc between the contributor and the reporter, since if you swivel the mic by rotating the pole on its axis, as opposed to moving it through space, you alter its acceptance/rejection relationship (angle) to the background, and the intensity of the background sound alters. Thus, the listener hears a change in the background noise level each time the mic re-positions during the dialogue, and/or the dubbing editor finds an edit difficult or impossible to conceal.

Add-ons

There's always an add-on you can get to help you out of sticky situations, and for pole operation, there are a couple that may make your life easier in the

Figure 27.2 The gun mic is held vertically between interviewee and interviewer, and the pole is pivoted (swung) between the reporter and the contributor, ensuring the mic remains in the same (i.e. vertical) plane. In this way, the relationship between foreground dialogue and background sound is maintained

circumstances outlined above. Depending on the 'reach' necessary for the shot, you may like to use a body 'harness' that lets you steady the pole in a 'stirrup'. Thus, you wear both the mixer and the stirrup.

Providing your mixer has the facility, you could use a remote fader attached to the pole which controls the gain of a channel fader (usually channel one). In this way, you can leave the mixer (on the ground/table/trolley, etc.) and hold the pole whilst standing closer to the contributors, controlling the gain if necessary via the fader on the pole.

Choice of pole
Which one do you need? It's almost like asking which size of screwdriver should you buy, no single one covers all eventualities. They come in many weights and sizes, comprising two, three, four (and sometimes more) telescopic sections. They need to be sturdy and lightweight, and not transfer handling noise to the mic. However, using a bass cut of 4 dB often improves the mic input by lessening the handling noise.

Although you would normally wind the mic cable round the pole, taking care not to leave slack that might flap against it and cause noise, there are poles available which have a tail at the top, to connect to the mic, and an XLR socket in their base. Many modern poles are carbon fibre, often with felt, or similar fabric, covering the outer base tube, and these tend to be the lightest weight.

They may be prone to sticking, however, and since they're also relatively expensive, many opt for a metal pole, when funds are limited.

Me and my shadow

The main curse of the pole is when it throws a shadow. That's what the cameraman says, of course the recordist knows it's the lighting that's caused the problem. Unfortunately, if the light happens to be coming from the sun, low in the sky, then it's not always practical to reposition the camera simply to eliminate the shadow, because 'That's the shot!' Or it may be lack of space on a location that forces the cameraman to place lights in positions which throw unwanted shadows the minute you put the pole in place. Under these circumstances there's usually no choice but to revert to the ubiquitous clip mics.

28 Sound recordist operation: multiple contributors

How many people can you cover on a single camera shoot? Unfortunately that's the sound equivalent of the 'How long's a piece of string?' question. You often find that, in spite of having advised a production concerning the limitations of a four channel mixer, on the day, several extra guests materialize, 'We just couldn't say no, and their views are vital, darling!' Yes, I forgot to mention that you must carry a large hat from which you pull rabbits several times a day!

Depending on the content of the shoot and the positions of the contributors (and the size of the shot/s and the acoustic, etc.) you may be able to cover everything and everyone with the gun mic on the pole. If there's a main presenter/reporter, you could put a (radio) clip mic on them, and use the pole for the rest of the contributors. Or if two or three of the guests are the major contributors, you could mic them individually, and again use the pole for the rest. You need to be sure that your results will be sufficiently flexible for post-production.

Therefore, before you start shooting, advise production that the limitations imposed by four channels may mean having to retake parts of the item to ensure intelligible sound throughout. During recording, if you do miss the beginning of someone's speech, it's normally better to wait until the end of the take before you ask if that particular answer is important (without the contributors overhearing your conversation) to give production the option of going for a re-take.

Multi-channel desk

Of course, providing you have advance information you may opt to use a larger mixer (Figure 28.1) and extra mics. If you do, (a) it could well require mains power, and (b) of necessity you'll be seated (recordists always get to the chairs first) in your own working area (check that there's sufficient space available at the location).

Should mains power (or lack thereof) be a problem, you could cascade the output from your portable mixer into one channel of another. Two four channel mixers then provide you with seven mic inputs. This is probably simpler than using two portable mixers and feeding the output of one to track one and the other to track two of the camcorder, although that would provide you with eight mic inputs. However, it's not an operationally portable option, if you see what I mean, and you still need an area to call your own in which to set up. Moreover, this tends to be a solution of last resort, as two portable mixers are difficult to control with a lively seven way (or more) discussion. With the left hand (and fingers!) on one mixer, and the right on the other, you'll find that split brain becomes more likely than split track!

The sound trolley

Rather than having to search for a desk or table (or other flat surface), working from a trolley affords much greater flexibility for your operation, especially when

Figure 28.1 Multi channel mixer

moving between locations. There are many available for this purpose, allowing you several options as to how you may best configure it to suit any given circumstances. For instance, you can choose the number of shelves, and where you place several other facilities on board. There's a wide selection of these which may be vital to your shoot, including mini-monitor, mics, DAT recorder, handsets, cables, dry cells, etc.

The base can be an ideal place to house large batteries to provide power (very often a car battery or two, depending on the length of your shooting day and estimated power drain), and many recordists utilize the trolley structure to clip the pole to the side, together with radio mic receivers (strapped/gaffered/clamped on to an elevated spare pole or stand, firmly attached to the side). Add to this all those other items from the mixer pouch I've already mentioned, together with a folding chair and thermos, and you'll never go back to working without one!

Mic stands

Years ago, it was a customary wheeze to send new recruits on a quest to technical stores for a long stand. But like screwdrivers, there's no single one (long or short!) that suits all occasions (Figure 28.2). When choosing a stand, you must ensure that it holds the mic stable and securely in the position you require. If it has a boom arm and/or telescopic sections, you must check that the arm/sections can be securely tightened to support the weight of the mic (plus windshield?) that you intend to use, and that they aren't prone to droop or collapse under the strain.

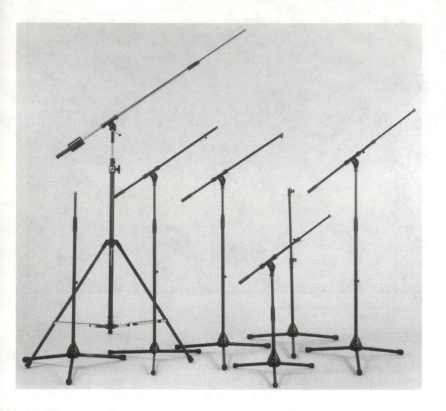

Figure 28.2 Mic stands (Courtesy of AKG Acoustics)

In use, they should be sited as safely as possible, and acoustically isolated from the surface on which they're placed. *Do not* use them on rough ground, or other unstable surfaces, unless you have a secure means of anchoring them in position. A heavy base is an asset, as are sandbags placed on the base, but these alone should not necessarily be relied upon as the sole means of anchorage. On exterior locations, I have seen stands roped down to tent pegs, and I recommend you use a minimum of three, which are best sited equidistant between each leg, if the stand has a tripod base. (But beware the possibility of noise being transmitted via the taut ropes to the stand, and thus to the mic output, especially if they get knocked by passers-by or buffeted by the wind, unfortunately, there's no perfect answer in atrocious conditions.)

Beware, the higher you raise a stand, the less stable, as a structure, it becomes overall. So even indoors, with no howling gale surrounding you, as well as weighting and/or securing the base, you may also have to put some form of 'protection' around it in order to prevent the possibility of someone getting too close to it and knocking it over. This protection should take the form of good solid structures, most locations should have suitable furniture such as desks or tables you can use for this purpose (you definitely don't want to carry these around with you). Note: avoid using chairs. I've often seen chairs placed round equipment to keep it clear of people, but I'm afraid that people more often than not remove those same chairs to sit on, leaving a potential accident exposed.

For cables, use the clips on the stand if they are provided, and double check the safety of the cable runs back to your operating position. Should the public have access to the location at any time during your operation, all cable runs should be secured using gaffer tape or rubber matting on the floor surfaces, or by correctly supporting and slinging them above the working area to avoid a hazard. When there are only members of the production on site, it is often assumed that they are sufficiently experienced to avoid the trip hazard presented by cables. Nevertheless, the safest course is always to secure them whenever possible.

Equalization

Multi-channel mixers generally have several other facilities available on their control panel apart from a fader per channel. Depending on the make and model, they can allow you to perform all sorts of sound manipulation or 'enhancement', the most common being EQ, equalization. Using this, the frequency spectrum is divided into bands, each one with controls to increase or decrease (amplify or attenuate) that particular portion of the spectrum. In this way you have more precise control over, say, the bass cut of a hand-held mic, or enhancing the bass response of a clip mic.

Should you be recording a musical item, for example, you might decide to use EQ to 'improve' one or more of the performers or their instruments. I would caution you against too much signal manipulation 'in the field' where listening conditions may not be ideal. Any signal processing of this sort is best left to post-production, especially if the signal is digitally encoded prior to recording.

Face the music

Whilst on the subject of musical items, you should confirm with your cameraman that he/she will not stop recording, even whilst changing shot and/or moving from one position to another, especially if he/she is shooting with the camera hand-held/shoulder mounted. This is most important as in these instances you must always ensure that the sound track is continuous. I promise you it's blood on the cutting room floor otherwise, as discontinuous music tracks are an editor's nightmare.

I haven't said anything about how best to place your mics for musical items, it's even more of the 'How long's a piece of string?' question, but one with knots in! In a handbook of this nature, nominally about single camera acquisition, I can but offer guidelines. First of all, are you only using the two camcorder tracks or do you also have other tracks separately available? The answer to this question obviously affects which decisions you can leave for the dubbing mixer/editor.

One mic

In the main, it's simplest to use only one mic, the gun mic for preference. Most musical groups/performers are used to public appearances, and should be self-balancing, especially if they are acoustic/unamplified. If they have a conductor, a good starting place is to position the mic over (and possibly slightly behind) his/her head, allowing sufficient room for enthusiastic arm movement, three metres clearance should be about right. Hopefully, you'll have time to rehearse, and adjust the position of the mic to bring about the desired result. If you've time, record the rehearsal and replay it to the performers, they may wish to adjust their performance/balance to improve the overall sound.

If the group uses amplification, you'll probably need to position the mic as far from their loudspeakers as possible, and hope that the overall mix sounds correct. Again, record a rehearsal, and replay it. With an enthusiastic (over-amplified) group, it will be almost impossible to assess their performance *in situ*, so replaying it in a quieter environment afterwards is vital. They may, or may not, be able to adjust their overall mix to the loudspeakers, and you may be able to convince them that for your purposes, it's best if they adjust the mix to ... and this is where your diplomacy may be stretched to its limit, or beyond, but suggestions are – bring the vocal forward, lessen the bass, back off the drums, shoot the pianist – no sorry, wrong script ... and hope that they comply.

With a multi-channel mixer, you may be tempted to use a mic for each instrument and/or performer, and even utilize separate recorders to provide extra tracks. This is only for the experienced recordist. The major problem you face is getting sufficient separation between the outputs of individual mics/tracks. If you don't succeed, there will be too much 'colouration' on some or all of the tracks from adjacent performers/instruments to enable the dubbing mixer to perform a satisfactory balance.

Shooting from several camera positions

Whilst on the subject of performance, should you be involved in coverage of on-stage activities, such as drama and/or musical items, you may very well find that the method of coverage from a visual point of view requires shooting the scene from several camera positions. In this way, there will be a reasonable variety of shots of different sizes from several angles, which will ensure flexibility of choice in the edit suite.

From a sound point of view of course each time you run the sequence, you'll have a different sound track (although this naturally doesn't apply if you're working to a backing track). And you must ask yourself, 'Which track is likely to be considered the main one?' before you actually run to record. I'm sure you'll soon realize that the shot which is critical to having the sound absolutely in sync with the vision is the close up, either of a character speaking, or of an instrument being played.

Therefore, make sure that any tracks shot in close up are *continuous* from a sound point of view, *especially* if the cameraman decides to move the camera at some stage during the performance, and even if he/she chooses a different shot size from a fresh angle. In other words, under these circumstances, the camcorder must *always* be running to provide a continuous track, regardless of the pictorial content (unless of course you're also running a separate sound recording on DAT, or similar, which you must keep running irrespective of what the cameraman is up to!). It may be that a sound edit can take place later, between two or more of your 'close-up' tracks, but do take care to ensure the consistency of your balance between takes for close-ups.

If time is available, you may also wish to re-run one or more of the close-up takes with a slightly different balance, bringing that performer/character a little more to the fore in your mix (see also Perspective below). Again, the more choice you can give the editor in post production, the better, but do ensure that each take is labelled or identified accordingly, as to any change you make to the mix or balance.

Perspective

Whilst it's unlikely you'll find yourself working on a full scale drama at the start of your career, dramatic reconstructions are often included in documentaries, and you must become familiar with working to a script. Whilst intelligibility is paramount, you must also match the sound perspective to the shot. For this it's vital that you have the camera's output on a monitor in front of you, together with a copy of the script, marked up in such a way that it provides you with a guide to the shot sizes applicable to different sections of the dialogue.

Obviously, if you have a CU of a performer, you want the sound to be 'close'. If on the other hand you're recording a WS, you'll want a more distant sound with a reasonable amount of surrounding atmosphere. If you're uncertain as to how the resulting recording is to be edited, you might decide to split track, and use close mic technique for dialogue on one track, and feed 'loose' sound to the other. This enables the dubbing editor to control the amount of background atmosphere in the final mix. But always check with the director/producer (or dubbing editor) beforehand as to what form of post-production may be applied to your results.

Communications

The sound recordist is usually tasked with providing communications, if required, on location. Whilst it's something else to bring with you, and check beforehand that it is fully functional, by providing it you remain in control of all the sound on location. You will almost certainly find it to your advantage that, however many handsets production request you to supply, it always pays to have at least two or more spare. In this way, you have one for yourself, and at least one spare for when one of the others gets lost or broken, or is required by the executive producer who's decided to drop in to 'see how things are going'.

Ensure you have plenty of charged batteries, and a *reliable* system of identifying which are charged and which are flat. Handsets which work with pluggable headsets (Figure 28.3) should help to cut down some of the extraneous noise generated by voluble production staff, and you should always endeavour to provide these in addition for each handset. One point to beware of though, the output from these handsets is easily swamped in a noisy environment, and tends to distort if the volume is turned up too far in an attempt to overcome the surrounding noise (even when used with a headset).

Figure 28.3   Radio communication handset (walkie-talkie) with headset

Working with assistants

A trained, experienced assistant is worth their weight in gold. Not only do you have someone to help with the overall operation, plus rigging and de-rigging, but you also have someone with whom you can discuss the minutiae of the sound coverage, and thus solve potential problems in half the time.

Communication is all-important, and you must keep them informed of all relevant information with respect to imminent changes, e.g. any deviation from previous plans/script. If they're operating a pole, and wearing headphones, they can all too easily miss production conversations leading to these changes, which may involve contributor or camera movement, differing emphasis in delivery of the dialogue, etc. Similarly, they are your eyes and ears if your operational position is out of sight of the action. They can pass messages via the mic to keep you informed of ongoing discussions concerning the shots amongst the camera crew, for example.

PA

Again, whilst you're in charge of all sound on location, you may be asked to provide an audio feed for PA. Depending on the complexity of the event you're covering, you may simply wish to select some feeds to an auxiliary output from your mixer. This assumes you don't have to adjust their level once set, or that the level you're using for your recording is also satisfactory for the PA.

However, more often than not you'll find that your programme mix is unsuitable for an audience feed. There are many reasons for this, an obvious example being if you only intend to record part/s of an event, and maybe record interviews whilst other aspects of the event continue. This being the case, you should supply a dedicated mixer and operator/assistant to take care of the PA separately, whilst you concentrate on your own recording. This probably also means that they will need separate access to your audio feeds, which may result in you having to supply DAs to provide these extra facilities. You'll need to liaise closely with them to ensure that the sound from the PA loudspeakers is not going to adversely affect/colour your own output.

On the other hand, if you need to obtain a feed from on-site PA facilities (over which you have had no planning or control), you may need to route it via a DI box (see Section 9, Mics: cables and radio; Direct inject box) in order to ensure you have a balanced feed.

29 Stereo: mics and placement

Stereo acquisition should not to be undertaken without forethought and planning. There has been much discussion/argument/disagreement amongst professionals over the best way to handle stereo acquisition on location. It mainly centres on the relationship of the sound to the picture. Shooting a sequence, the viewpoint/camera angle changes between each shot; the burning question is – should the sound perspective change to match the visual perspective of each frame? A simple example (as transmitted on one Australian soap) illustrates what happens if we go down this road (Figure 29.1).

Shooting singles of the characters with the mic positioned as for a monaural recording, the fountain switches sides on each cut. This will both draw the viewer's attention to the mechanics of the edit, and prove extremely disconcerting.

Sound stage

At present, custom and practice favours establishing a 'sound stage' for each scene, usually as if viewed square on to the action. Before shooting, you must agree with the cameraman and production where this 'front of stage' line is going to be drawn. If the camera crosses this line, the left and right of the sound stage will appear incorrect, even though the camera has not technically crossed the visual line (which can all too easily shift angle/position with artist movement).

On location, dialogue is recorded in mono, and in post-production is placed into an ambient stereo atmosphere corresponding to your sound stage. Using a pan pot, the dialogue may be shifted left or right as desired within the overall image. It cannot be over-emphasized that you *must* know how your results are to be used in order to provide both sufficient and effective material to 'build' a believable stereo image. This obviously means that you must record sufficient ambient sound track (without any over-obvious aural intrusion/s, i.e. 'noises off') at your location into which the mono dialogue can be placed (see Wildtrack, below).

Sound bite

If, for example, you can be certain that only a sound bite (that is a single unedited clip) is being used from an interview, you could use a stereo mic over the camera to cover the interviewee, and place them in the middle of the sound stage. A similar situation may pertain for a PTC or vox pops (but *do not* consider giving a stereo mic to a reporter to handle – see Don't move! below). Once recorded in this fashion, using a pan pot will essentially only be able to shift the *whole* image left or right.

Wildtrack

The problem with using 'true' stereo on location is being able to ensure sound continuity over any edits, especially if portions of the sound image (people, vehicles, etc.) are on the move – imagine the amount of wildtrack you'll need to successfully cover all the joins. On a stereo shoot, you need to cover every

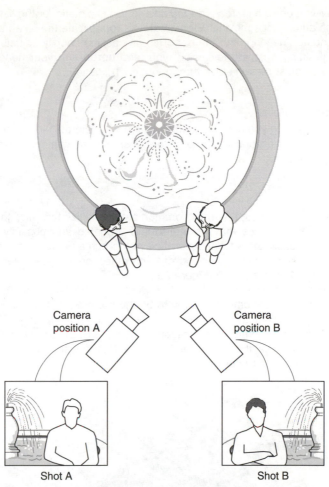

Figure 29.1 The two actors are seated in front of the fountain; but when the cut is made from one camera to the other, the fountain switches from one side of frame to the other in the background and its sound 'ping-pongs' from left to right

eventuality from every angle (staying the same side of your 'front of stage line'), and easily record three or four times more wildtrack than you would on a mono shoot, from each position. A separate sound recorder is virtually mandatory, e.g. DAT.

Don't move!
The first time an experienced recordist uses a stereo mic on a pole, and obeys his/her instinctive reaction to quickly move the mic to follow dialogue, you'll see their face turn green, as their world literally revolves around their ears!

Whatever you do with stereo, you *must* keep the mic static, or the listener will notice the aural image moving. Stereo sets out to replicate the binaural experience of human hearing, and the ear/brain processing happily adjusts to head turns, but sitting watching television, you tend not to turn your head, so the sound stage must remain static throughout each scene.

On camera mic
From the foregoing you can deduce that mounting a stereo mic on the camera is impractical for acceptable sound coverage should the camera move or pan/tilt in any direction.

Mics
Since we have two ears, the most common set-ups utilize two mics to achieve the desired result. Mics may be individually mounted and possibly spaced/angled to represent the spatial separation of the human ears, or they may be mounted piggy-back fashion on top of each other, or both capsules may be contained within one housing (Figure 29.2).

For simple location use, the first set-up would be considered impractical, and one of the other two methods is likely to be the preferred option. Although the obvious way of recording stereo is to record left and right information (A/B) on two tracks, it's more common on location to record M/S, especially for dialogue, as with the mic correctly placed this has the added advantage of providing a strong mono signal for later use.

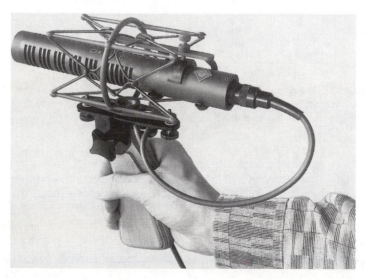

Figure 29.2   A hand-held M/S stereo mic (Courtesy of Neumann/USA)

Middle or main and side (M/S)

Middle (or main) and side: a directional mic capsule points forward and a figure of eight mic capsule collects sideways information. The combination of these mics provides Sum and Difference signals, which are the two recorded sound-tracks. Thus the 'Sum' signal is a ready-to-use mono signal, and the stereo information is in the 'Difference' signal, which needs to be decoded along with the 'Sum' for stereo sound. A/B stereo signals, left and right tracks, can be obtained from the M/S signals with the correct equipment and conversely, M/S is readily obtained from A/B signals.

The two modes are directly related (simplistically A+B=M and A–B=S), but if the image is wrong in one, it will be wrong in the other, there's no magic 'fix-it' in post-production. However, when using M/S you can widen your image by increasing the S signal relative to the M. However, the S signal *must not* be greater than the M signal, and you run the risk that if your image is too wide, information that is clearly heard in stereo is lost in mono (it's a bit like viewing an original 16×9 picture transmitted as 14×9 protected, you can't see the edges of frame!). A centrally placed source should give a zero S signal, whilst a source panned fully to one side should give equal M and S signals.

Pole operation

On location, mic handling techniques for stereo are radically different from mono. Although you will certainly be using a mic on a pole for some, if not all of the time, due to the mic's construction/sensitivity this will almost certainly be more prone to handling noise from the pole than the equivalent mono operation. Check the mic on the pole for unwanted/unexpected noise before you venture into the field, you may find you need to obtain a different pole.

Of course, you'll want to maintain a steady, not to say as static a mic position as possible, but there may be circumstances that force a repositioning of the mic whilst recording. If you set the acceptance angle of the mic to wide (in visual terms, using your lens, it's the equivalent of zooming out) then any slight move-ment will hopefully be imperceptible to the listener – but do be aware of the compatibility of the mono signal! If the visual analogy helps, shot development on a wide angle lens is less wobbly and distracting than shooting on a narrow angle.

Having set your sound stage, do give a thought as to whether you're working the pole over or under the action. In mono, recordists often swap the 'above or below' mic position between shots with gay abandon, but if you do so working in stereo you will obviously laterally reverse the image, unless you change left for right. In A/B you can do this by swapping the inputs to the mixer, or in M/S, you can phase reverse the S signal.

30 Stereo: mixer

Ganged controls

Operationally, when you use two channels ganged together on one fader to control the overall level of the stereo signal, you must also ensure that the limiters on both the channels are ganged. Should this facet of the operation be overlooked then, if one channel is louder than the other and peaks to a level where it 'hits' the limiter whilst the other does not, there will be a shift of sound image.

Additional mixer stereo facilities

All incoming sources must be in phase, and to overcome any problems you should always carry at least one phase reverse cable, although the mixer will almost certainly provide a switchable phase reverse on at least one channel. Other facilities available with the mixer should include the ability to change A/B inputs to M/S, and vice versa, with appropriate monitoring. There may also be controls on the mixer to vary the 'width' of the mic input. Stereo mics tend to take more power than mono, so batteries won't last as long using phantom power via the mixer; do make sure you carry sufficient spares.

Cabling and identification

When cabling to the camcorder, most recordists adopt the convention of colour coding: red for left (track 1) and green for right (track 2). It is essential to double check all your connections to avoid any possibility of confusion at a later stage. More importantly, note on both cassette box and label whether you've recorded M/S or A/B. Verbally identify the beginning of each cassette (after bars and tone) with the same information, or add this information to the clapper board if one is in use, just to be on the safe side.

Levels

Another area where there is a variance of opinion amongst professionals is the preferred recording level, complicated by the need to provide a mono-compatible signal (a good reason to use M/S on location). A full consideration of this subject is beyond the scope of this handbook, but to minimize the possibility of hitting limiters (not ganged!) in the camcorder chain, it's probably safest to under-record by at least 3 dB. Therefore, line-up tone should be no higher than −20 dB on the bar meter, and preferably below, some recordists opting for as low as −24 dB. Stereo tone will ident at least one channel, the simplest ident being a cut in the left channel, and should always be used to indicate a stereo signal.

The mixer should have good quality meters (often two PPMs) but these take experience to read and interpret for stereo signals. It is not always easy to determine that you are providing the desired output, since they give no hint of phase errors for example. Remember, if you're monitoring M/S, the S signal will be much lower than the M signal. Listening to stereo on headphones on location also takes experience to recognize the desired levels and any discrepancies that arise due to phase errors.

More often than not, the quality of meters on camcorders leaves something to be desired, another reason for erring on the side of under-recording your levels. Since the spectre of unreliability rears its ugly head, especially where onboard limiters are concerned, for any stereo production you should insist on recording on a separate broadcast quality recorder, such as DAT. Or you can use a mixer with an onboard hard disc recorder. In both instances you can revert to recording a reasonable signal level, and leave the camcorder tracks solely as a back-up and editing guide.

Mono compatibility

If you are recording in stereo (as opposed to mono dialogue to be placed in an ambient sound stage), you must separately monitor all sections that require mono compatibility. When you hear individual performers within a stereo image, their position within that image assists in defining their contribution, but in mono, their rendition may simply 'blur' into the whole of the aural surround. The visual equivalent is the difference between colour and black and white framing. In colour a person wearing red clothing will easily stand out from a blue background, but in black and white the two colours may simply merge together in similar shades of grey. So, for mono compatibility, as with black and white, you must monitor the whole in that medium.

31   Live broadcasting

There is a certain adrenalin rush to going live, as it's when your 'It'll be all right on the night' assurances are put to the test, and any mishaps are immediately transmitted to the viewers. However, you, as the sound department, need not only to handle the sound output from your mixer, but also check the circuits to and from base, and ensure that you are both sending the required level and receiving the correct feeds from them.

Links vehicle

More often than not, you will be working into a separate vehicle which provides the link to your base via satellite, microwave, fibre optic, or ISDN. It's always advisable to know which methods of link are in use (some locations may require a combination) as it might affect the availability of some of the reverse circuitry, and/or cause delays in the signal path. The engineer on board will establish the link and may also handle all the identifications and deal with the correct provision of your talkback, etc.

They will expect to receive your output (probably on XLRs) and will provide you with incoming feeds, possibly on break-out boxes, or you may be handed one box connected to a cable loom into which you plug your output and select the relevant communications facilities from its various outlets.

Communications

Depending on the complexity of your OB, and the facilities available via the links vehicle, there are a number of communications facilities you may require from base.

■ *Omni (or open) talkback*

Continuous talkback straight from the control room or gallery has the purpose of controlling and co-ordinating the live broadcast. Programme sound is often heard over omni talkback from loudspeakers in the gallery.

■ *Switched talkback*

This is only operative when switched by the producer/director in the gallery. Switched talkback is usually required by the presenter on site, so that they only hear specific instructions in their earpiece. On a complex OB, with more than one presenter, you may require more than one independently switched talkback feed.

■ *Reverse talkback*

This is a switched talkback from your OB back to the gallery, for use either for engineering purposes, or for a Floor Manager. You will almost certainly need a talkback box on a flying lead for more complex operations, and you should always have the means to provide it as an emergency spare even if you have:

■ *Radio talkback*
Obviates the need for wires strewn about a location, and allows greater flexibility for all concerned. The frequency in use must be licensed (via JFMG in the
UK), and can suffer from RF problems as outlined in Section 9, Mics: cables
and radio; Radio mic rules. The other problem with radio talkback is that it tends
not to perform well in extremely noisy surroundings, and is liable to distortion if
the volume is turned up too high. (Hence the need for the cabled standby, as
mentioned above.)

■ *Clean feed*
The overall programme sound mix fed back to you *minus* your own output
(known as *mix* (or mixed) *minus* in the USA). This obviates any of your contributors hearing themselves whilst speaking (highly off-putting, even for professionals), and overcomes echo effects from circuit delays. Do *not* confuse
this facility with foldback, although itself a selective feed, which you do not want.

'When are we on?'
Omni talkback is vital in conveying decisions reached in the gallery as to the
timing of any live event. The less control a programme exerts on an event, the
more likely changes necessitate altering the time and duration of your on-air
piece. For this reason, many experienced presenters prefer to have omni talkback in their ear piece, so they're aware of last minute decisions which, in the
heat of the moment, may inadvertently not get passed on to them via switched
talkback. The downside is that they may hear themselves when you do go on-
air, but they accept that and have learnt to mentally 'turn it off'.

The gallery may frequently ask what's happening at your location, and whilst
you're not on-air, the answer can be passed via your main sound output. Quite
often the gallery wish to converse with the presenter, and listen to his/her
answers via their pre-fade. Once on-air, questions from the gallery can only
safely be answered on reverse talkback, do *not* use mobile phones!

Circuit check
When circuits are being established, the normal signals sent to line are bars
and tone. Many bars generators these days have the facility for adding a text
identification, but to confirm that your signal is the one being received, it's
standard practice to cut to 'ident.'.

Cut to ident.
If you are cutting your outgoing tone, it should be done in conjunction with
reverse talkback or a phone connection to base, so that you can verbally confirm the moment you cut and restore your signal. Normally you would do this
two or three times, saying 'Gone, back, gone, back ...' as you cut, until base
confirm they're receiving the correct signal (you can often hear your signal
cutting over the talkback/phone circuit).

Similarly, you may need to ask base to identify the various talkback and
clean feed circuits to your link/OB, and this is done in a similar manner.

However, for ease of identification, outgoing circuits from base often have a tape loop playing on them, for example 'This is the clean feed circuit from Studio A to New Leaf OB'.

Be aware that if you're working on a major event, especially with several other sources feeding into base, a general election, for example, you may be asked to identify your outgoing circuit several times, and probably immediately before you go live. Don't assume because you've done it once, it won't happen again.

By the same token, with major events you need to keep an eye (ear?) on your incoming circuits, since with the ongoing havoc and chaos which frequently surrounds live broadcasts, last minute re-plugging and re-scheduling at base may inadvertently re-direct your circuits elsewhere.

On-air

In a well-ordered universe, you will have been given a clear indication of your precise on-air time, and the expected duration of your contribution. Back in the real world, assuming the omni talkback remains clear, you may be given ample warning and precise cues, or you may simply hear the strangled cry of 'We're on you . . .!'.

The worst case scenario is losing some or all of your reverse circuits, and having to rely on an off-air feed to cue your contributors. Should this happen, you may find that the only indication you have that your own output is still being received at base is when you get 'cut to air'. This is probably the *only* time I'd recommend having a mobile phone in use, to find out what on earth's happening! But do *turn it off* once you're on-air, and have established that everything is sorted.

Whilst every OB should have an off-air vision feed available, under no circumstances should you allow off-air sound to be fed to loudspeakers or a presenter's earpiece on site. Quite apart from the possibility of putting the presenter off their stride by hearing themselves, you'll almost certainly get a howl-round of mammoth proportions[1], and necessitate base or the network cutting away from you forthwith. No matter how it occurred, you'll shoulder the blame!

So, even if members of your on-site production team ask for programme sound to be fed to a loudspeaker for the benefit of contributors or guests, *insist* that they listen via headphones or earpieces away from the action area, preferably via a distribution box (and/or use a parallel box which has one input, either jack or XLR, and several jack socket outputs for headphones) over which

---

[1] Unless you're live to air via a satellite, which can introduce a delay of up to two seconds. It eliminates the possibility of a howl-round, but if a presenter has programme sound in their earpiece (against your advice, naturally), even though they are used to hearing themselves, the second/s delay could render them speechless!

Should you have sufficient equipment and time at your disposal, you could feed incoming comms via a second (small mono) mixer, and provide an on-site mix of talkback. In this way, when your presenter is talking, you fade down the studio sound, and fade it back up after their reply, so that they can hear the studio.

you have control of the volume. Having insisted of course, you may be expected to supply headphones and/or earpieces, so you should check when receiving a booking for a live broadcast whether this facility is required.

It is good working practice to carry spare headphones and earpieces, but if you do, also ensure that you have disinfectant wipes to clean them before and after use. Professional presenters have their own moulded earpieces, but you will have to provide the necessary lead and feed for them. They never carry a spare, and you will be their hero forever if you can provide them with an emergency spare when theirs fails!

Standby (hot spare)

Speaking of emergencies, always have *at least one* line-fed standby mic plugged, especially if you are using radio mic/s for your main sound. Depending on the event, your decision will probably be between using either a reporter's hand mic or a gun mic.

Live – from a phone near you!

There are various computer based devices available that allow you to send sound and vision via a phone (landline or mobile, although the latter is *not* to be recommended, as has already been mentioned, once or twice) or ISDN line in real time. At present, the quality, due to the compression rate applied to the signal, is not up to broadcast specifications. However, because of their portability, they're being utilized more and more for ENG work, especially on assignments abroad.

The more sophisticated devices allow you to work at different resolutions (variable signal compression), depending on the frequency spectrum available for your transmission, i.e. phone, ISDN, LAN or satellite. Thus, several data rates are available, and if you have sufficient bandwidth, you can send a broadcast quality signal in real time. Another option open to you is to send uncompressed full broadcast quality sound and pictures down a phone line, but not in real time. A typical data transfer rate for a phone circuit at present is in the order of forty minutes on-line required to transmit one minute's worth of sound and pictures. Whichever option you choose, the base to which this data is sent will obviously need to have the relevant software installed to interpret the signal.

32 Digital sound

Today, virtually all recorded signals are going to enter the 'digital domain' at some stage. It is beyond the scope of this book to explain the 'mechanics' of this process in any great depth, but a simplistic overview may help you understand where potential problems lurk.

'The greatest invention since sliced bread'

A sound signal is a continuous and, for other than a steady tone, varying voltage (Figure 32.1). The first assumption in digitizing is that if you 'look' at that voltage once every 'xth' fraction of a second, and if 'x' is sufficiently small, replicating those values of voltage sequentially every 'xth' of a second thereafter will be indistinguishable, by ear, from the original continuous signal (Figure 32.2). Imagine a thinly sliced loaf of bread with every alternate slice removed. If the remaining slices of bread were to remain upright and in place, when viewed at an angle, the eye might be fooled into seeing a complete loaf.

The second assumption is that by 'chopping' the 'columns' of voltage up into a sufficient number of steps or levels and by assigning a numerical value of one 'bit' to each level, reproducing these values will again 'fool' the ear into hearing a continuous signal (Figure 32.3). Thus, the digitization process requires a sampling rate (every xth of a second) and a quantizing level to produce each 'sliver' or 'column' of signal. Imagine a child's building blocks. With the correct measurements you could easily replicate the height and outline shape of your own house, or car, or any other structure you care to name. But by now, you'll appreciate that you need lots of columns of blocks to faithfully reproduce these shapes. The same goes for digitizing, we first have to establish the parameters that will give us a sufficient number of 'bits' to faithfully replicate a signal without seeing or hearing the individual 'blocks'.

So the quality of the reproduced signal relies on the number of samples per second and the number of quantizing (or digitizing) levels. The sampling rate

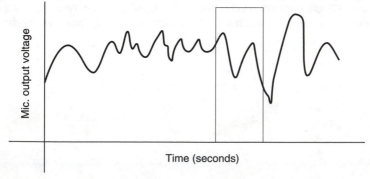

Figure 32.1 The analogue sound signal

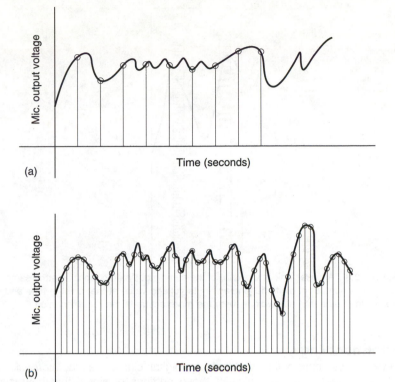

Figure 32.2 (a) The signal sampled at regular intervals, but in order to accurately represent the original, the sampling rate (every 'xth' of a second) must be at least twice the highest frequency that you wish to record (b)

must be more than twice the highest frequency to be reproduced, and the quantizing level must be sufficient to replicate a smooth sine wave (e.g. as produced by your tone oscillator). These factors determine the number of 'bits' the system must handle in real time.

Having done this, you're recording digital data – 'ones' and 'noughts'. Every time the signal is reproduced, it's a 'clone' of the original, there is no perceptible loss in quality. However, to reduce the amount that has to be recorded, many systems compress the data. This is fine for one pass through a codec, which seeks to restore the signal to its original analogue values. But if the signal passes through a series of codecs, with different compression algorithms – for example, a signal path that consists of being recorded on tape or disc (first codec); transmitted via satellite (second), received and stored on a computer's hard disc (third); edited with software on a desk-top machine (fourth); and finally transmitted digitally from the server via a further compression system for both sound and pictures (fifth) – you can see how errors get the chance to multiply.

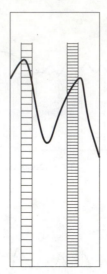

Figure 32.3 A closer look at a portion of the sampling. When quantizing each sample is assigned a number of digits depending on its voltage value at that point in time and the greater the number of steps/digits (bits) the more accurate the representation

Error handling

Nevertheless, anticipating problems in digital signals, extra information is added to assist the restoration of those portions of signal that have been lost. Error correction can reconstruct the digital signal *exactly* providing enough of the original remains intact (Figure 32.4). If errors continue to mount, error compensation interpolates (guesses) lost bits and reconstructs a 'probability' of the original signal. Too much 'guessing' leads to the picture displaying 'blocky' areas in frame (Figure 32.5) and some strange audio transitions or a 'cracky' or 'gritty' aspect to the sound.

The worst case scenario is when the errors exceed the capability of the system to interpolate, and the whole signal simply vanishes (Figure 32.6). Essentially, with a data stream of 'ones and noughts' you're dealing with on/off states, and a lack of sufficient information equates to off. This is both the strength and weakness of digital systems, their ability to handle errors and restore lost information is good, but when a problem overcomes this ability, the signal is lost in its entirety, and if the signal path is complex, it may take a long time to find and eliminate the fault.

Figure 32.4 Error correction reproduces a perfect picture

Figure 32.5 Error compensation, too much 'guessing' leads to 'blocky' pictures (and 'gritty' sound)

Figure 32.6 Too many errors overwhelm the correction/compensation system, result – no picture (or sound!)

33 Timecode

More often than not, part of the recordist's job is to set timecode. There are certain conventions to be observed when doing so, and you should always check with your production team (or the editor in post production) to find out which option/s they prefer. At present, most NLE systems need to 'see' continuous timecode, and can become upset if it is discontinuous, i.e. if it suffers from interruptions, which can more often than not interrupt any digitization of the rushes at that point. So care must be taken if and when you (or the cameraman) rewinds/reviews/replaces tapes and/or changes battery to ensure that you reset exactly to the *end* of the previously recorded material before recommencing recording (see also Timecode on location, below).

With broadcast camcorders, there is a choice of information you can lay on to the tracks associated with timecode (Figure 33.1).

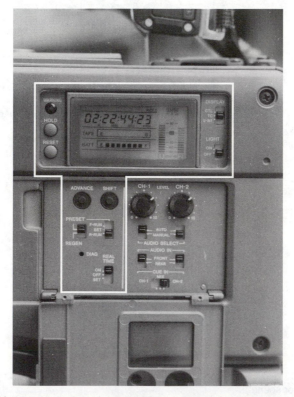

Figure 33.1 Various timecode and data options can be set via the switches on the panel under the LCD display

Control track

This track is the electronic equivalent of sprocket holes, and assists the replay machine to synchronize correctly with the recording. It is essentially a counter, utilizing hours, minutes and seconds (and on broadcast camcorders it often also registers frames, thus HMSF in total), but merely registers control pulses. Should you reset it in mid cassette and rewind your tape, it will return a negative value. (Care should be exercised if you have this function selected *during* recording, as pressing Reset – also see below – will instantly zero the display.)

Caution

It is erroneously referred to as timecode in basic DV systems, which only have this facility to indicate elapsed time, thus it is unlikely to be frame accurate on a replay machine, once removed from its original recorder.

Data or U-bit

Data, or user bits as they are labelled on some camcorders, is the equivalent of an identification stamp. Being a hexadecimal display, it can be set to any value from zero to nine and A to F. It remains permanent/static throughout a recording, and tape review, eject or insertion, until manually reset. If you wish to use this facility, always set it before setting timecode, since its 'set' position freezes both functions.

Timecode

It's probably easiest to think of this as a digital stopwatch (displaying HMSF), which you can either start and stop with your recording (R-run), or continually run showing time of day (F-run), the LCD display value of which is then laid down whilst recording. Upon replay, whatever has been recorded on this track will be displayed on the replay machine's timecode reader, and will be frame accurate.

Many non-linear editing systems require that this track be numerically continuous, thus R-run is chosen. In any event, you must ensure that any discontinuities in timecode or the process of recording material over several days/tapes does not result in the same code being recorded on more than one cassette. To avoid problems with a discontinuity, run for a minimum of ten seconds before allowing action to commence, and note this timecode on the cassette label and box.

Hold and reset

There are two buttons associated with timecode. Hold simply freezes whichever display is selected, although the data continues to be updated in the background and is once again displayed when Hold is released. Reset is used to zero the display (whilst in the Set mode), for example when you change a cassette.

For precise setting information refer to the camcorder handbook. Broadcast camcorders also have a function to allow time of day to be recorded in Vertical Interval Timecode (VITC).

Timecode feed to ancillary equipment

You will need a cable to connect with the Timecode out BNC socket on the side of the camcorder to the relevant input (refer to handbook) on the ancillary equipment. To ensure precise locking, the lead needs to remain in place throughout recording (see Radio timecode below).

Feeding timecode in the opposite direction, from ancillary equipment to the camcorder, is not recommended. For example, you may have a backing track of a performance on tape (e.g. DAT) with timecode reference. By feeding that to your camcorder you match the timecode to the pre-recorded track. But, each take will generate exactly the same timecode, a post-production nightmare unless this has been agreed beforehand, and the takes are digitized separately. It may then prove beneficial to have the same timecode for ease of synchronous shot editing, but do ensure that this is indeed the requirement before you undertake the assignment.

Radio timecode

There are several systems available, but any problem in signal path or battery failure will result in gaps/errors in timecode, providing post production exasperation. A more secure cable-less system is the use of Lockit Boxes, see also Section 22, Sound recordist operation: mixer; Mixer/recorder.

Timecode on location

If you rewind your cassette to review earlier shots, you must be careful when re-setting the tape that you don't over-record previous material, unless this is intentional. This is because, having rewound the tape, when you next run to record, *irrespective of tape position*, TC resets itself to the number recorded at the end of the previous final take, and runs from there.

Let's take an example, with a new cassette loaded, zero the timecode, and start recording. Having reached 00.12.08.04, the director wishes to check a previous shot for continuity. You rewind and replay the master shot which ends at 00.05.59.22. The director is satisfied with continuity, and yells, 'Run to record,' as time is tight. However, having finished replaying the tape, you'll notice that the timecode once again reads 00.12.08.04 with the tape stationary, even though you haven't played or spooled forward to this point. Do not make the mistake of thinking that the tape has magically jumped forward, and for goodness' sake don't start recording immediately! Press Return (Ret) on the lens (or zoom demand) to review the last few seconds of the tape, and the timecode will once again run up to 00.05.59.22, but when the tape stops, it resets to 00.12.08.04. Your choice is to spool to the end of the recorded shots and reset at the end of the recording, or to alter the TC setting if you really intend to over-record from 00.05.59.22.

By the same token, should you wish to record on a partially used cassette, having found the end of the previously recorded pictures, you may wish to reset TC and CTL. Replaying the end of the last shot will display the previously recorded TC. When the tape stops, however, the TC display will revert to the value it displayed prior to the insertion of the cassette. To avoid confusion, I would always leave some seconds difference if I entered fresh TC information. For example, assume the end of the previous recorded pictures is 00.12.08.04. I would not set TC to 00.12.08.05; rather I'd add a few seconds, or more likely round up to the next minute, and start recording from 00.13.00.00 (but make a note on the cassette label and box!).

However, most of today's digital camcorders have a timecode Regen function, which regenerates the correct timecode from the inserted tape. Switch to the Regen position and replay the last few seconds of recorded material, and the timecode will be reset from off-tape information. Using the Ret button on the lens to replay and reset on the last few seconds of the previous recording, you can also ensure that timecode continuity is retained for editing purposes. This also applies to the previous example of over-recording material. Set to Regen, and the timecode will reset to the value it picks up from running a few seconds of pre-recorded material. You can then begin to record from that point onwards, and the timecode will be continuous. However, the dangers of misusing this facility cannot be over-emphasized!

As already indicated, you cannot reset CTL to follow on from previously recorded information, nor does the LCD display a previously recorded value. You either leave the information as it's displayed – i.e. whatever it was prior to inserting the cassette – or simply zero it. But you must run-up for at least ten seconds to provide a safety margin for post production requirements. If switched to CTL position, selecting Set will re-select TC, and TC values will then be displayed and altered by the use of Advance and Shift, or by pressing Reset. The CTL value will remain unaffected, and the display will revert to CTL when Set is deselected.

Head cleaning

The 'quality' of LTC (longitudinal timecode) and Control Track can be affected by the state of the heads in the audio stack, which records their data. Should the head become clogged, or worn, the strength of the recorded signal may be insufficient to correctly register on a playback machine. Regular maintenance should ensure you don't encounter this problem.

More information

A detailed article by the author on timecode use and setting, including synchronizing several cameras, is to be found in *Zerb* 50, Summer 1999, also reprinted in *Image Technology* July/August 2001, Volume 83, No.6.

34 Pre-location equipment check

To simplify the chore of gathering together all the equipment you need before a shoot, you should prepare an itemized checklist of tasks and equipment (preferably at least a day beforehand) whilst referring to the requirements listed on the call sheet. On the shooting day itself, always allow time to reassure yourself that your equipment is functioning as it should before leaving your base, especially if it is drawn from a pool of equipment used by others. Equipment supplied by a third party (for example, a client or hire facility) for the shoot should be itemized on a separate list, and should always be checked before you set off for location.

Sound-wise, if you do nothing else, ensure that before you leave base:

- The on-camera mic is working and providing sufficient level.
- You can monitor its output on both headphones and the LCD meter display.
- There is no interference/noise on either channel.
- You are able to record and replay 'clean' sound on both tracks satisfactorily.

You should also refer to the check lists below for single person operation and sound recordist operation.

Test tape

To ensure that the camcorder is fully functional, have a test tape prepared which has both sound and pictures recorded under controlled conditions to use as a reference. Before you leave base, insert the tape in the camcorder, and compare the camera output to the pictures off tape on a broadcast quality monitor (I suggest that amongst the test video signals on the tape you use a known quantity such as a good quality colour photographic print which you also place in front of the camera – do the outputs match?).

The tape should have a minimum of one minute of bars and tone to check the meter line-up, plus sound recorded in a known acoustic environment (if you can manage to acquire clean studio sound, it is an excellent reference source). Listen carefully to the sound output on both a loudspeaker and via the camcorder monitoring circuit on headphones, and ensure that they both sound 'clean', i.e. no appreciable noise or interference is present on either. I'd also advise you to take the test tape with you on location, in case you find it necessary to re-affirm the camcorder's performance.

Equipment list

Remember to take your itemized equipment list/s with you (arranged so that the contents of each case or bag can be clearly seen at a glance). It not only means that you can check whether you have all you need before you depart, but also simplifies the task of undertaking a 'wally' check before you leave each location (that's scampering around everywhere you've been shooting to make sure you haven't accidentally left anything lying around).

Having a preferred method of arranging your equipment whilst loading and packing your vehicle also helps you to verify that all has been safely and securely stowed.

Single person operation
Check:

- Are all your batteries charged and individually labelled?[1]
- Do you have sufficient fresh tape stock?
- Is there any visible sign of damage to the equipment?
- Does the test tape sound (and look) all right?
- Do your headphones work, do you carry a working spare?
- Have you set the correct monitoring level?
- Does each mic work (including the on-camera mic), do they have windshields?
- Can you access each channel/track?
- Are the sound levels correct?
- Are all your cables/connectors working (give each a good waggle when plugged-in)?
- Is the camcorder recording and replaying satisfactorily (plus all the other vision checks: viewfinder, lens, exposure, colour balance, etc.)?
- Is the timecode properly set?
- Is your kit bag packed (refer to Equipment list)?

Sound recordist operation
Any and all of the above checks that apply, plus:

- Is your mixer fully functional?
- Is the metering accurate?
- Do you have sufficient means to power it for the duration of your shoot?
- Do you have all the mics you need, does each sound OK?
- Radio mics, have you the correct frequencies, does each work at a reasonable distance, have you sufficient spare dry cells?
- Audio cassette recorder and cassettes.
- Earpieces and wipes.
- Other ancillary equipment specific to the shoot.

[1] In order to cycle through re-chargeable batteries efficiently and, therefore, ensure each is used as regularly as the others, it is advantageous to label/identify each one. This additionally assists you should one prove problematic on location, since batteries are one item that get bundled willy-nilly into a kit bag during the wrap, and sorting out a faulty item from amongst the rest at base is difficult without an easy means of identification. You should also have a system to indicate whether batteries are charged or uncharged (if there is no indicator built into the battery).

35 Fault finding

The suggestions for fault finding below rely in your confidence that all is working perfectly before you leave base (see also Section 34, Pre-location equipment check). Nevertheless, faults can show up when least expected, and knowing how to work through the equipment in a logical order can help pin down the offending item, and may hopefully provide an instant solution, such as a switch incorrectly set. Sections 3, Camcorder: audio facilities; 4, Camcorder: track selection and magnetic recording; and 7, Camcorder: external facilities, are set out in a logical working and plugging order, and reference to these sections should help, in addition to the following suggestions and reminders.

Power

If everything appears to be dead, check your battery condition and connection. On some models, it is possible to accidentally knock and disconnect the battery when plugging cables at the rear of the camcorder. Batteries themselves can break internally (especially if dropped) and still appear perfectly all right from their external appearance. Some batteries have fuses, which may also 'blow' if too high a power drain is placed on the system (the most common example being the use of an on-camera light of too high a wattage). If the LCD display does not register characters, check/change the battery. The display probably also indicates the charge status of the battery as a guide (see also Section 7, Camcorder: external facilities) but you should carry several batteries as spares/back-ups in case of unforeseen problems (when other people lend a 'helping hand' it's all too easy for batteries to be left on location, in taxis, in coat pockets which are then left in a cloakroom, etc.).

If changing batteries proves ineffective, it is conceivable that the battery mounting plate may have developed a fault, and you will need to provide power via the 4-pin XLR socket, usually sited at the rear of the body. You can either use a mains adaptor which provides the correctly polarized 12 V DC for the camcorder, or an adaptor lead from a battery to the 4-pin XLR socket. If this too does not yield results, there is a cut-out designed to protect the camcorder itself from overload or power surge. It is frequently sited towards the rear of the body, and it may need to be reset.

If the equipment has separate replay functions, ensure it is switched to camcorder. On broadcast equipment, ensure that you have not selected the save (or cam) mode, when the tape will not be in contact with the heads, and no sound will be apparent on any monitoring facility.

Sound metering and monitoring

Assuming that the camcorder is powered, and that there is no sound signal apparent on either sound channel via your headphones or the meter display, first switch the track selection from the rear inputs to the on-camera (front) mic.

Does the camera mic work, i.e. produce a signal? Switch to auto level to ensure the problem isn't an accidentally knocked level control.

This gives you a starting place, especially as you confirmed that it was working before you left base. At this point, we'll assume that the camera mic is producing a signal, so the fault lies somewhere on the input side of the selector switch. Do ensure that you can both hear the camera mic via your headphones and see its signal displayed via the metering.

If the metering is working, but your headphones are dead, with camera (front) mic selected to both tracks one and two, check:

■ Are they correctly plugged into the camcorder body? Pull the lead out and push it back, several times if necessary, to ensure it's properly seated in the socket. The jack socket itself may be faulty and not making proper/full contact with the plug.
■ Is the mini-jack damaged (the most common fault on headphones)? Waggle the lead close to the socket connection, to see if there is a cable or wiring fault. To be 100% sure, try the headphones in something else, for example, a personal stereo/cassette player.
■ Is the headphone lead damaged or broken at the headphone end? Give it a good waggle around the headset/each earpiece.
■ Is the headphone monitoring level (on the side of the camcorder body) turned up to a sufficient level?
■ Do the headphones have a volume control in their lead? (Turn it fully up, and tape over it.)
■ What have you selected via the audio monitor switch? Toggle the switch through its positions to eliminate the possibility of a faulty connection.

If none of the above produce results, plug in your spare set of headphones and repeat the process.

Sound signal chain

Assuming your headphones/monitoring are working correctly, switch back to the rear inputs, and work through your cabling and plugging – mic to camcorder – in sequence:

■ Are the cables fully plugged into your mic/s and the camcorder input/s? If in doubt, swap the leads over and/or check with a spare lead to eliminate cable faults. Waggle each cable end whilst monitoring for a signal.
■ Is phantom power turned on if it's necessary?
■ Plug up a different mic, especially a dynamic mic that doesn't need power.

Work back through the routing:

■ What is selected to channel one?
■ What is selected to channel two?

Check settings for front/mic/line and attenuation, if necessary. Switch backwards and forwards through the switch positions, the selector switch may be faulty/dirty. If you have plugged in a mic, check that mic/rear is selected for that channel.

For plugged mic channels, switch rec. level to manual, on both channels, and adjust gain/levels on the two circular dials labelled CH-1 and CH-2 whilst monitoring on headphones (the potentiometers may become 'dirty', especially if used in the same position with one mic for a long period of time and lose signal, turn them backwards and forwards several times to 'clean' them, and have them maintained as soon as possible). Is the channel one gain adjustment on the camera body turned fully up? The bar graph on the LCD display is a very rough guide, be confident on how it sounds on the headphones, if it sounds right, it is right. Sound at too high a level is also indicated by the limiter light, red LED, flashing (not DV).

If there is *no* signal, check to see that nothing looks broken, you'd remember if the equipment had been dropped/knocked between base and location, I'm sure. If there is a signal, but the camcorder won't record, check that the cassette is record enabled, i.e. that the red marker hasn't been accidentally pushed in/slid to one side. Moral: do not re-use cassettes.

Noise

There is a signal from your mic/s and the meters are working, but you can hear a noise/hum/buzz in your headphones, 'Where's it coming from?' you moan (usually loudly). First check your headphones by swapping them for your spare pair, is the noise still present, and at the same level/amount? Faulty headphones may produce a loading or mis-match on the monitoring circuit, producing a hum or buzz.

If the noise is still present, switch your monitor to channel one only. If the noise disappears then the problem may be on channel two. If the noise is still present, turn the channel one gain control up and down, does the noise level alter? If it does, then there is a problem with this channel (always assuming the problem simply isn't distortion caused by over-modulation, i.e. the gain turned up too high, but you'd see that on your meter, unless it was faulty). Alter the channel selection switch between on-camera mic and rear input (try it quickly several times to ensure it's not a faulty/dirty switch). If the noise is on both positions, it may be a monitoring fault. If it's only present on one position, then that is where the problem lies, change the mic or cable and/or turn the phantom power on and off.

If the noise persists after all your switching and re-plugging, it may be an internal wiring fault/dry joint/failing amplifier, or it may be a signal (RF) induced in the cable. Re-plug a spare mic on a short cable directly into channel one. If the noise disappears, then it is probably caused by induction on the mic/cable combination and/or routing and/or a cable fault. Make sure you do not run your sound cables close to mains power/cables. If the noise persists, you will have to avoid using the faulty mode, and feed sound with the switch selected to the non-noisy input.

If necessary, undertake the same procedure for channel two. Hopefully, you should have now managed to pinpoint the fault.

Noisy monitoring

If, after undertaking all of the above checks, you can still hear noise, it may actually only be present on the monitoring circuit. Check this by inserting your test tape, and replaying a section of known quality. In all likelihood, if the noise persists. it is only the monitoring system at fault, but you should have the rushes checked as soon as possible on a player. If you can immediately send one off to an edit suite for a check, so much the better. If you have no test tape, then your only safe course of action is to find a way of replaying a tape on another player to ascertain if the fault is being recorded.

Intermittent noise

Intermittent noise may be caused by faulty wiring/cables/connections, or it may be induced from some form of RF transmission. Culprits are:

- Mobile phones (ensure everyone on location turns theirs off! Switching to silent/vibrate is not sufficient, they MUST BE OFF).
- Radio and/or TV transmitters in the vicinity.
- Radar.
- Magnetos (especially on board boats).
- Large plant or machinery with electric power switching.
- Electrically driven/operated vehicles, for example, fork lifts, milk floats, etc.

Need I say, radio mics are especially prone to these sources of interference (see also Section 9, Mics: cables and radio; Radio mic rules). You will need to move sufficiently far from the source of the interference in order to proceed, unless you can simply turn it off for the duration of your recording. Having said that, moving your receiver closer to the transmitter may also eliminate the problem, but if you do so, be aware that this may only prove to be a temporary fix. If the problem itself is due to a moving source, this could again come closer to your operating position and re-generate the fault.

36 Equipment

Throughout your career, you will acquire many items of equipment, ranging from the marginally useful ('I can't imagine why I keep carting this around') to the absolutely vital ('Where the – expletive deleted – is it, I distinctly remember putting it in the kit?'). When you do purchase your own equipment, make sure you keep any equipment manuals in a safe place, and photocopy the parts you most often use for reference and carry them with you if necessary.

If you have several items of one type, e.g. rechargeable batteries or XLR cables, it is good working practice to have them individually identifiable. In this way, you can for example establish a routine for cycling through the batteries, ensuring each gets regular use; and should problems develop on location, faulty items can be easily identified when you return to your base.

If anyone else uses your equipment (even a producer or director listening on headphones for a few minutes) always check that it is still working correctly before you pack it away at the end of the working day. You should also establish a routine for regular equipment maintenance.

Headphones

Without a doubt, the one item you MUST have is a pair of headphones, and you should take a reasonable amount of care when choosing your own pair. Your decision will in the main depend on the types of location and shoot you undertake on a day to day basis. Unfortunately no one pair will be right for every location, although after a couple of years, you'll probably own several pairs anyway. The points you should consider when purchasing your main pair are:

- The quality of sound reproduction. You can only tell if your sound is of the highest quality so long as your headphones are capable of faithfully reproducing it. Seek professional advice from other sound recordists, and be prepared to spend a reasonable amount of money.
- For the majority of location applications, you'll need 'open' headphones that allow you to hear some peripheral sound, as opposed to 'closed' cans which seek to minimize this. Alternatively, should the environment be extremely noisy, then you may find a pair of closed headphones are preferable. However, in these particular circumstances, depending on the noise level, and assuming you're simply trying to ensure intelligible speech, you may find that a small pair of ear phones worn under ear defenders would be your best option.
- Working single person operation, you may prefer the option of a single headset to cover one ear only.
- You will have to wear the headphones for long periods of time. Ensure the ones you choose are comfortable.
- The ear pads on headphones often wear out, and/or become dirty. Ensure you choose a pair that have easily removable pads for cleaning and/or replacement.

- Always carry a spare set. In an emergency, a cheap lightweight headset can be a lifesaver. They have the added advantage of being available for production use.

Basic tools

A very personal choice, but the most common, and vital are:

- Screwdrivers – pack of jewellers with both cross head and flat blades.
- Multi-function tool – a Swiss army knife or Leatherman (or a sharp blade/penknife at minimum).

Kit bag

There is a vast range of bags to choose from, look in any photographic shop for an everyday run bag, with:

- Both a (comfortable) shoulder strap and carrying handle/s
- Waterproof
- Padded
- Containing moveable internal sections
- At least a couple of exterior zipped pockets.

Heavier duty bags specifically designed for video equipment can be obtained from specialist video dealers, details of which may be obtained from professional organizations.

The following are close to essential to keep in it:

- Gaffer tape
- Range of dry cells (do not buy too many at once, unless you use them frequently, as they have a finite shelf life, and it would be foolish to find all your batteries expiring at the same time).
- Audio cassettes
- XLR cables
- Spare windshields and clips for radio/clip mics
- Phono cables
- Adapters
- Test tape
- Pen and/or marker
- Torch (at least one).

Plus of course, whichever mics you're using on the shoot, together with their windshields and clips.

Also useful:

- Crocodile clips
- Sash cord
- 4-way mains socket and RCD
- Head cleaning tape
- Fuses and fuse wire.

Extra tools

Many sound recordists are dab hands at performing running repairs on equipment. There's nothing worse than having a whole shoot come to a grinding halt simply because a plug has come off a lead, and you've no spare. Consider the following as part of a professional outfit:

- Soldering iron (and/or capable of 12 V operation on location) and solder
- Wire strippers
- Test meter
- Insulating tape.

Accessories *in extremis*

Depending upon the location, and the conditions (weather) and other unforeseen circumstances under which you're operating, you may find the following items useful/essential:

- Earpieces
- Antiseptic cleaning wipes
- Parallel boxes (for feeding several headphones/earpieces)
- Hairdryer (speeds up equipment drying-out process)
- Direct inject box (balance transformer)
- Blu-tack
- Clear sticky tape
- Plastic bags (waterproof)
- Pouch/es for radio mic transmitters
- Battery charger
- Handsets (walkie-talkies) and their chargers
- Thick rubber, for use under stands
- Rubber matting, to cover cable runs
- Whistle
- Cotton wool
- Needle and thread
- Adhesive Velcro pads/strips
- Safety pins
- Tissues and toilet roll
- Toupee tape
- Drapes
- Folding chair
- Condoms (non-lubricated, waterproof).

XLR cables

Since these are available in different colours, and/or with different coloured glands, I'd advise having as many colours as possible, since it assists with identification. For the professional with the wire strippers and soldering iron, XLR cables should be wired to the IEC standard, X = external – pin 1 – ground: L = live – pin 2 – live signal/hot: R = return – pin 3.

And the rest ...

Were all this not enough, you'll almost certainly find yourself being asked to carry various items of equipment for others, such as video tapes and camera batteries (essential if you're working by yourself!). In which case, you'll probably find that two medium-sized bags are easier to manage than one big one (and you may occasionally manage to persuade a colleague to lend a helping hand, especially if your gear comes in easy to handle pieces – see also, Flight cases and packing, below).

Mixer, pole and mic stands

Are considered in Sections 22, 27 and 28, Sound recordist operation: mixer; pole operation; and multiple contributors, as is the use of a sound trolley in Section 28.

Hire

No matter how much you own, you're eventually bound to find yourself working with equipment belonging to the client/broadcaster, or hired for the shoot. When you collect the equipment, make sure you obtain a list of every item, together with any reference or serial numbers. This will assist you to avoid the possibility of overlooking anything when you return them, especially if they are in your care for several days or more.

Whatever you do, always treat equipment with respect, especially if is not your own. Should you find it to be faulty, report the fault to the owner as soon as possible (you certainly have no choice if the fault has brought the shoot to a halt). When returning faulty equipment, ensure you attach a label/note briefly outlining the fault, place it so that it cannot be missed when the equipment is received at base/hirer's, and notify them by phone at the earliest opportunity.

Flight cases and packing

- All equipment should be fully protected for travel.
- Pack in logical order, with equipment for immediate use on top for easy access.
- Soft bags are good for in car and around locations, but not for airlines, as baggage handling can be severe, expect dents in cases.
- For practicality, it's best to have two or more medium cases (easier to carry, and more flexible to stow in hired vehicles, which are always smaller than you wanted) than one/two big ones (too heavy), but it's advisable to check with the airline before travelling with regard to excess baggage, do they assess it by weight or number of pieces?
- If you are carrying rechargeable batteries, travel with them charged, and split them between cases, if you have more than one – this helps spread the load, as they are often heavy, and should the worst happen, and one case goes missing, you have at least some means of powering your equipment

- Select sturdy cases, well padded, with lots of foam in the interior – many of the specialist cases available allow you to fashion your own interior from the segmented foam.
- Gaffer tape over the exterior clips/securing straps/locks to protect them from damage/accidental opening, and carry a roll of gaffer tape separately to re-seal after customs inspection.
- Depending on the countries you intend to visit, you may find it invaluable to have the facility to lock each case.
- Label and number each case.
- Keep a list of the cases together with a guide to the contents of each, it's useful both for inspection by authorities, and for assisting in your re-packing at the end of a shoot. Take several copies of your equipment list with you (including serial numbers and item values). You will need this if you are using a carnet, and it is always useful to have it for your own records.

Camcorders should be hand carried at all times, albeit in some form of easily portable protective bag/case. For ease of stowage in aircraft overhead lockers you may choose a bag/case which more easily contains your equipment if you remove the lens (but use lens caps), viewfinder, mic (if removable) and battery and pack them around the camcorder body. It is always advisable to keep these items with you, together with a cassette in the camcorder for minimum shooting requirements, in case you should encounter any problems with lost baggage at your destination.

Vehicle

Your vehicle should not carry any distinguishing marks or logos if you intend to operate in sensitive areas. It should have an alarm system fitted, and if it's an estate, it should be fitted with security locks on the tailgate and a security cage in the rear compartment (check your insurance requirements against these items). In the event of an accident, the security cage prevents the equipment in the rear of the vehicle from being catapulted into the front passenger area, minimizing serious injury. Whatever your vehicle, *never* carry large, heavy or bulky equipment in the passenger compartment, always ensure that it is stowed safely and securely within the cage or luggage space.

The vehicle should also contain:

- Fire extinguisher
- Road maps
- First aid kit.

Establish a routine service/maintenance schedule for your vehicle, and be pre-pared to hire a replacement when necessary.

Add-ons

Whatever equipment you use on a day-to-day basis, whether hired or owned by your client or yourself, you're bound to find that after a while it doesn't quite work the way you'd like, or that some of the switches or other functions/controls could be better sited for your purposes. I've already mentioned that many recordists are dab hands with a soldering iron, and frequently make up their own 'bodge-boxes' and similar devices, which can often take on the aspect of reject props from a sci-fi shoot.

If these items are completely stand-alone, all well and good, but some of these 'boxes' may require mounting on, or close to, other items of equipment. When the equipment is your own, you may treat it as you like, but I must reiterate what I said before about treating other people's equipment with due care and respect. Seek permission before you add *any* extraneous items adjacent to, or on top of a third party's equipment. You may only be using gaffer tape to attach it, which you may reasonably expect to be pretty simple to peel off after a shoot. But it only has to become damp (accidentally) and you can be left with some form of mark or mess on the equipment body, which may be difficult to remove satisfactorily.

The use of adhesive Velcro strips or patches to attach small, lightweight items to equipment makes for a tidier and more professional look to the combination overall. This is also a better option to take if the attached item has to have a dry-cell changed at regular intervals (or any other internal switching), as it's much easier to remove and replace quickly.

But those Velcro patches are there for all time, and you do *not* want to stick them on equipment in a position whereby any woollen clothing (or similar material) will come into (permanent!) contact with the patch/strip. Of course, you will have made sure that the Velcro 'hooks' are on the small item to be attached, not on the main equipment, but in my experience, the patches that are left 'bare' still attract any stray fluff/hairs, etc. in the vicinity. So, if you do utilize this method of attachment, at the same time as you stick the original item on the equipment, have made up a flat plastic or thin metal Velcro-backed item of the same dimensions to place over the patch/strip on the equipment, for when the additional item is not in use.

37 Mics: technical information and operational summaries

A microphone capsule translates the energy from sound waves into an electrical signal. It is said to be pressure operated when the sound energy impinges on one side of its diaphragm, the other side being enclosed. When the diaphragm is open to sound waves on each side, it is said to be pressure gradient operated. The latter type tends to be more sensitive than the former, but the signal produced is lower, and thus needs a greater degree of amplification.

Moving coil
Its 'ear' is a diaphragm attached to a coil of wire 'suspended' within a magnetic field, and the energy from sound waves moves the wire within this field, thus generating (inducing) a small electric current across the coil. Hence the electrical output is derived solely from the energy imparted by the sound waves. The mic does not contain an amplifier, and so its signal output is lower than that of amplified (condenser) mics, requiring greater amplification at the camera/mixer (Figure 37.1).

Condenser
This type of mic is a variable capacitor (condenser), and requires power for its operation. Sound waves impinging on the mic capsule cause one of the plates of the capacitor (the diaphragm) to move, thus varying its capacitance. This change in capacitance across the plates is 'seen' as a small varying voltage which is then amplified at the mic head. This pre-amplified signal is passed back along the cable to the camera or mixer, where it requires further amplification prior to recording (Figure 37.2).

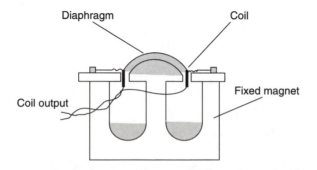

Figure 37.1   Moving coil operation

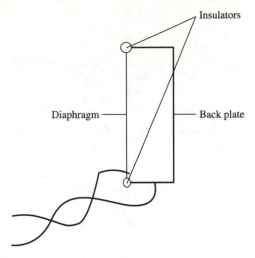

Figure 37.2 Condenser operation

Electret

Another form of condenser/capacitor design, working on a similar principle, but the capsule (ear) carries an electrostatic charge, which is sealed into the unit during manufacture. This design makes possible a very small capsule size which in itself does not, therefore, require power to energize the capacitor, but does require power for a head amplifier. Clip mics have a thin cable from capsule to head-amplifier and power pack. The output signal strength is similar to the condenser mic, and still requires amplification at the camera/mixer.

Figure-of-eight polar diagram

For M/S stereo, most mics in use on location consist of a combination of a cardiod and a figure-of-eight capsule. The polar response shows why it is called a 'figure-of-eight', as this capsule 'hears' best along one axis (which can either be considered front to back, or in a stereo sense, side-to-side), with very little pick up at 90° to this axis (Figure 37.3). The cardiod capsule captures the forward sound (providing the M signal) and the figure-of-eight provides the S information.

Mics: operational summaries

Stick (omni, dynamic)

Pros

- Good quality sound.
- Rugged/robust, no handling noise.
- Doesn't need power.

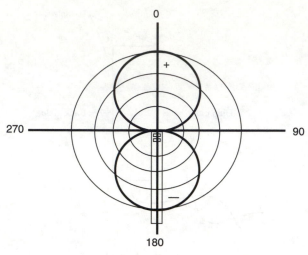

Figure 37.3 Figure-of-eight polar diagram

Cons

- Lack of sensitivity (due to lack of head amplification).

Gun
Pros

- High quality.
- Directional, helps minimize unwanted sound.

Cons

- Bulky, if used with windshield.
- Needs careful handling.
- May not function well when wet.
- Needs power (not necessarily a problem if phantom power is readily available).

Clip
Pros

- Can be relatively close to required sound source.
- Small and light, easy to carry.

Cons

- Personal jewellery, clothing rustle, head turn off mic.
- Wind noise.
- Needs power (not necessarily a problem if phantom power readily available).

Radio
Pros

■ No cables.

Cons

■ If using a clip mic, all relating to it, plus:-
■ Correctly siting the transmitter, receiver and aerials – line of sight transmission.
■ Maintaining batteries.
■ RF interference.
■ A licence is probably required.

(Figures 37.1, 37.2 and 37.3 are reproduced from *Multiskilling for Television Production*, P. Ward, A. Bermingham and C. Wherry, Focal Press 2000.)

38   Call sheet details

At a minimum, the call sheet should provide you with sufficient information to arrive on time at a given location with the necessary equipment, together with a list of the people involved in the shoot, their function and contact numbers. Nevertheless, it's often useful to have other details concerning your location, and a well-ordered call sheet will contain all you need to know about shoot/ times/location/security/hazards/facilities/directions, etc. etc.

For some shoots, much of this information will have been put together from a site visit by production. On complex shoots, there are times when you may be invited to join in this location visit to assist with the planning. In order to pass the relevant information on to your colleagues, I suggest you take a copy of this list with you.

Location planning – recce
You need to ascertain the following:

■ The full postal address of the location, including postcode. (An O.S. reference is useful for remote locations, and/or a photocopy of a local map, with the site marked in highlighter.) Directions to site are a bonus, but must not be substituted for the address/postcode.
■ Names and telephone numbers of on-site contacts/PR.
■ If permission is required to shoot anywhere on the location (or any particular insurance provision necessary), how may it be obtained, from whom – name, position/designation and contact number, and how long will the process take? (See also, Accreditation/passes/permits, below.)

Make sure you have the details for all three sections above in writing.

As well as obtaining the following details, it is useful to mark, or indicate their position on a site plan:

■ Parking should be arranged as close to the shooting area on the site as possible for all vehicles carrying equipment. Remember to make provision for the time involved in loading and unloading. If at all possible, obtain parking space/permits for all vehicles involved in the production
■ Security and ease of access to the site/building – will equipment movement in and out prove straightforward? Points to note are:
  ▪ Are the entrances/doors/corridors sufficiently wide for manoeuvring the bulk of the equipment?
  ▪ Do stairs need to be negotiated, and are they of sufficient width?
  ▪ Are there (working) lifts with sufficient capacity?
  ▪ Are trolleys available?
  ▪ At (or just prior to) the call time, is there likely to be any difficulty with obtaining entrance?
  ▪ Will equipment or facilities be delivered to site before (and/or collected after) the scheduled on-site times? If so, are there facilities to store it securely overnight if necessary?

- Will either of the above cases pose a problem for any on-site security? Designate the person whose responsibility it is to notify them beforehand.
- Are there any other restrictions with respect to emergency access to the site?

■ Position of the shooting area relative to the compass – indicate north on sketches/plans, the cameraman needs the information to determine the position of the sun (which may be very important from a continuity point of view for previous shoot/s, scene/s).

■ Risk/hazard assessment – check that production complete the form, and ensure that all relevant details appear on the call sheet.

■ Indoors – points to note are:
- The room size, does it have alcoves or other raised or partitioned areas, its wall colour/s, ceiling height and colour, the type of floor and its covering and colour?
- The position of doors, their dimensions, do they open outwards or inwards, and are they designated fire exits?
- Windows (and skylights) – their sizes and positions, do they open, if so which way, and do they have curtains and/or blinds which fully cover their surface area? What is the position of sunlight (where's north)?
- The style and colour of furnishings and fabrics?
- Details pertaining to fixtures and fittings such as – the size and position of mirrors and/or glass fronted cabinets, the types of tables, chairs, cabinets, desks, shelves, wardrobes, etc. Are they easily moveable?
- The position and value of ornaments and antiques, can they be removed for the shoot, or are they a necessary part of the location/storyline?
- Acoustics – note the amount of reverberation, and whether there is any intrusive noise, such as ventilation, clock(s), fridge, phones, office equipment, etc. plus any disturbance likely from outside the room such as a reception area, public access, catering facilities, lift motor, kitchen, bar, toilets nearby (see also Outdoors).
- Room lights – how many are there, how bright are they (what sort of power), are they on dimmers, what type are they (chandelier/wall-light/ floor or table stand – are they tungsten/fluorescent – do they have coloured shades) and their positions?
- How much electric power is available (but do not simply count sockets/ outlets)? Check the amount of power/circuitry with on-site sparks, and make a note of their name, number and availability on the shooting days. Plan for cable runs to lights/equipment, taking care not to propose a route for cables directly across fire exits, etc.
- Where are the nearest fire exits?

■ Outdoors – points to note are:
- Sources of noise over which you have no control, and your proximity to them. Examples being, road/rail traffic, building/road works, emergency services (sirens), public clocks, church bells, airport, etc.

- Exterior lighting over which you may have no control, for example, street lights and floodlights. What are their position/s in relation to your shoot, how much light from them is likely to affect the location, and what type (colour) are they (important if night shooting is planned)?
- The prevailing weather conditions, what is the long range forecast, but irrespective of its prediction, always make provision for inclement conditions?

- Numbers – how many people are involved at any one time (both on camera and off, such as guests, advisers, roadies, supernumeraries, etc.) and are they all TV experienced? Are any of them likely to be unpredictable (children and animals spring to mind immediately)?
- Facilities – how close/accessible are toilets, food, drink, accommodation? Is public transport easily accessible, bus/train station, airport, taxi?
- Emergencies – location of first aid on site, local hospital, doctor, police station.

Events

Points to note are:

- Official start time – plus are there any proposed restrictions and/or security surrounding the event which could hinder parking, access, etc.? If so, what is the earliest time that they are likely to come into force?
- Accreditation/passes/permits – what type of personal ID is necessary? Is there paperwork to be completed on an individual basis? Are passes available to all those on the shoot? Do they provide access to *all* areas, and are they valid for the whole event (especially if it takes place over several days) or are there restrictions and/or different 'levels' of passes? If so, how many? Who is responsible for providing them (name/official position/number) and how long will the process take? How will the passes be collected/distributed?
- Formal attire – are there likely to be any important dignitaries and/or members of the royal family present? Is formal dress or other special attire required?
- The number of people in attendance – how many people/guests/audience are expected and will there be press and/or other crews present?
- Public address – is there PA, and will a feed be provided on request?
- Related or simultaneous events – will there be other activities/events taking place at the same time, such as a local carnival, competitions, celebrations, etc. which may cause travelling, access and/or noise problems? When forward planning, always keep your eye on the calendar for bank holidays, royal birthdays, Trooping the Colour, Remembrance Day, Bonfire Night, etc. which may place restrictions on your activities.

Crew call sheet

The call sheet should be easy to read, with important points in bold or large text. It should be printed in black type on white paper for ease of fax transmission. All times for the day should be specified using the 24 hour clock and local time.

Any travelling between time zones should be very clearly indicated. To provide an overall indication of journey time, include the time at your home base in brackets, e.g. arrive Paris 1630 local (1530 GMT).

The name of the production/client, the production company (together with the company logo), their address and contact numbers should feature prominently at the head of the document.

This information confirms the veracity of the booking, and also serves to authenticate your presence upon arrival at the location, should security or other staff require proof of your status.

Call time and R/V

- Crew arrival time, using the 24 hour clock, and (specific) meeting place on location (e.g. 0900: main reception).
- Full postal address including postcode.
- Names and telephone numbers of on-site contacts/PR.

Production details

- The names of the production team.
- Their base/office address and phone numbers and fax number if different from page heading.
- Their mobile numbers and home numbers.
- The details from the recce, hazards and precautions, plus 'Tech Reqs'.
- A brief résumé of the shoot.
- A timed running order for the day's events, covering rigging, shooting, meal breaks, travelling between locations, and expected de-rig/wrap time.
- Other relevant information, especially if other days or crews are involved in shooting for the piece/programme, plus any special requirements.
- Post-production schedule, VT/film editor's name/contact, and TX time/date.

This should be available to the crew at least 24 hours before the shoot.

The earlier the crew have the call sheet, the earlier they can ensure that the requirements – especially with regard to hiring/availability of equipment – are met. It also allows time for them to institute last minute queries arising from the information on the sheet.

Shooting

On the day

- Meet at the R/V as specified.
- If you were unable to speak to production beforehand – spend the first few minutes discussing the shoot. They should:
  - Outline the finished product.
  - Indicate whether there has been a previous shoot, together with details of shots which may need matching, and plans for future shooting with respect to the same item.

- Specify the order of interviewees and whether they are to be framed right to left, or left to right, where applicable.
- Provide details of shots/effects/problems specific to the location.
- Identify possible problems, e.g. interviewee availability, parking restrictions, site access, etc. has enough time been allowed overall, and is there any slack?
- Contingency plans, or where things may differ from plan.

Discussion beforehand minimizes the risks posed by potential problems which could disrupt the shoot.

- At the end of the day/shoot, ensure that production have all their tapes/rushes, and that they are clearly and concisely labelled.

TRIANGLE LINES

Shipping for Shooting

The Harbour, Port Haddock, Marineshire, UK
+44 000 000 000

PTO CRUISE

CALL SHEET
6th Day of shoot : 30th February 2003

Location :	On board SS Soundscape, moored in harbour, Port Haddock
On site contact :	Capt. Mugwash
	Mobile : 000 000 00
Parking :	All vehicles - Harbour car park
RV :	0730, Harbourmaster's office - for day's running order, see over

Production Office :	77, La Trine, Harbour Offices, Port Haddock
Phone/Fax :	00 000 000 000

Producer :	Amy Collins	M 0 00 00000	H 111 111
Director :	Molly Edmonds	M 0 00 00000	H 111 111
P.A. :	Cheryl Wright	M 0 00 00000	H 111 111
Research :	Paul Rollings	M 0 00 00000	H 111 111
Ltg. Cam. :	Chris Underwood	M 0 00 00000	H 111 111
Sound :	Adrian Moore	M 0 00 00000	H 111 111
Sparks :	Vic Beresford	M 0 00 00000	H 111 111

To shoot :	Scenes 23, 44, 62, 63, 66, 71, 74, 80, exterior boat deck
	Scenes 16, 18, 22, 27, 29, 31, 38, interior Bill's cabin

Weather forecast :	Showers, some heavy, sunny later
Sunrise / set :	0618 / 1740

Tech. Reqs. :	Standard Digibeta kit + jib arm, production to supply stock
	2 radio mics in addition to standard kit
	Standard lighting kit + 2.5 kW HMIs & generator

For emergency cover, first aid facilities, and post production schedule - see over

Figure 38.1   Specimen call sheet front page

39 Insurance

As a professional you will need to protect yourself against unforeseen circumstances which, assuming a worst case scenario, may result in a claim being made against you. Whilst individual requirements differ, you should consider all of the following, alongside advice from one or more of the relevant professional bodies, who may offer full or partial cover as part of their membership benefits, or provide access to a scheme at favourable rates.

You may find that some policies are only valid for certain geographical areas, and you must be careful that you are covered for every country in which you are likely to find yourself visiting/transiting/working.

Public liability
Ensure that you are covered in case your actions, or those whom you employ, lead to an accident in which people are injured, or property or valuables are damaged.

Employee liability
Protection against claims affecting those who assist you on location, even if you are not paying them wages.

Professional indemnity
Covers the liability of the insured for negligence on the part of themselves and their employees in the pursuance of their employment.

Equipment
If you own equipment, cover it against theft, accidental damage and hiring replacement equipment whilst repairs are undertaken. You may also wish to include cover for hiring extra equipment on a job by job basis.

Personal life
Check your policy for exclusions which may affect some of the work you undertake. Examples are, filming in riots and war zones, risky lifestyle activities, and flying by any means other than scheduled airlines. These contingencies should be covered by your employer, but do check that extra or alternative cover is in place before you accept these assignments.

Travel
Cover against delays and cancellations affecting your travel, and should include provision for accommodation and/or alternative transport if you find yourself unable to travel immediately to your next destination. But do ensure that you are fully covered for the purposes of your work/employment. Most travel policies are designed purely for holidays, and are almost certainly limited to a number of days in a specified time period (as well as geographical limitations).

They probably do not cover 'risky' lifestyle activities and sports, and you should take care when working/filming in this type of environment that the exclusion could also be applied to your activities.

Medical/health

When travelling/working abroad, some policies may be invalid for further travel/work abroad for a period of time after your return home. This is to cover their liability in case you are incapacitated by an infection/disease you contracted during your trip, which may take several days/weeks to incubate thereafter. Check your policy to ascertain the time limit imposed, and if you are required to work or travel abroad within this time limit, you will obviously need to provide yourself with alternative/additional cover (which, if consecutive trips abroad are for the purposes of work, may be provided by your employer).

Personal accident/injury

Cover for injury to yourself arising from an accident, which may have occurred either through work or leisure activities. These schemes often only apply after several weeks of incapacity.

Vehicle

Your vehicle should be covered for carrying equipment, employees and possibly artistes. You may also require your insurance to cover any driver with your permission. This need can easily arise, for example, if whilst on location, vehicles need to be moved, and you are unable to do it yourself whilst shooting. The most practical solution is to give your keys to the Production Manager, or other staff, to move your vehicle.

Income protection

This is an expensive option, but you may wish to consider it if you have dependants. However, if you do decide to go ahead with one, be very careful over the wording with respect to provision of benefit, as you need to be fully covered for any inability to do your full-time professional job. Some policies restrict their liability if you are able to function in any capacity whatsoever (what, still breathing?).

Appendix A: industry associations and societies

AES – Audio Engineering Society – www.aes.org
AMPS – Association of Motion Picture Sound – www.amps.net
APRS – Association of Professional Recording Services – www.aprs.co.uk
BECTU – Broadcasting Entertainment Cinematograph & Theatre Union – www.bectu.org.uk
BKSTS – The British Kinematograph, Sound and Television Society – www.bksts.com
CAS – The Cinema Audio Society – www.ideabuzz.com/cas
GTC – The Guild of Television Cameramen – www.gtc.org.uk
IBC – International Broadcasting Convention – www.ibc.org.uk
IBS – The Institute of Broadcast Sound – www.ibs.org.uk
JFMG – Joint Frequency Management Group – www.jfmg.co.uk
NAB – National Association of Broadcasters – www.nab.org
PLASA – Professional Lighting and Sound Association – www.plasa.org
Recording Arts Forum – www.recordingartsforum.com
SBE – Society of Broadcast Engineers – www.sbe.org
SMPTE – Society of Motion Picture and Television Engineers – www.smpte.org
STLD – The Society of Television Lighting Directors – www.stld.org.uk

Appendix B: bibliography

Bartlett, Bruce and Bartlett, Jenny. *Practical Recording Techniques*, Third Edition, Focal Press, 2001.

Eargle, John. *The Microphone Book*, Focal Press, 2001.

Grant, Tony. 'Zerb Basics – Timecode', *Zerb* **50**, Summer 1999, reprinted in *Image Technology*, July/August 2001, Volume 83, No. 6.

Nisbett, Alec. *Use of Microphones*, Fourth Edition, Focal Press, 1993.

Rumsey, Francis and McCormick, Tim. *Sound and Recording: An Introduction*, Fourth Edition, Focal Press, 2002.

Talbot-Smith, Michael. *Sound Engineering Explained*, Second Edition, Focal Press, 2001.

Uren, Martin. *BKSTS Illustrated Dictionary of Moving Image Technology*, Fourth Edition, Focal Press, 2001.

Ward, Peter, Bermingham, Alan and Wherry, Chris. *Multiskilling for Television Production*, Focal Press, 2000.

Watkinson, John. *An Introduction to Digital Audio*, Second Edition, Focal Press, 2002.

Appendix C: terminology

For a more comprehensive description of technical terms used throughout the industry, I recommend *The BKSTS Illustrated Dictionary of Moving Image Technology* by Martin Uren, published by Focal Press.

Glossary

1+1 – one plus one, referring to an interview, interviewer plus one interviewee (1 + 2, two interviewees, etc.).
2S – two shot, similarly 3S, 4S, etc.

A/B or **A and B** – left and right signals for stereo reproduction; or A/B – as before, depending on context.
Atmos – Atmosphere, the aural 'surround' to a location, often recorded as wildtrack, q.v.
Aux – Auxiliary.

Backing track – Pre-recorded track used for performers/contributors guide to re-creating a timed performance and to possibly add further/main sound track.
Bar meter – (or bargraph) usual LCD display of sound level.
BCU – big close-up.
Buzz track – see wildtrack (colloq.).

Cans – headphones (colloq.).
CF – clean feed ('mix/mixed minus' USA), part of communications, programme sound feed to location minus the location sound input.
Codec – coder and decoder.
Comms – communications.
Condenser mic – see Section 37, Mics: technical information and operational summaries.
Control track – series of pulses recorded on tape to enable replay machine to synchronize to the recorded signal. Counting the pulses and displaying them on a reader gives an output of HMSF (q.v.)
Croc clips – crocodile clips.
Cross talk – one signal interfering with another, usually via an induced electro-magnetic field in a cable or circuit.
CRT – cathode ray tube.
CU – close-up.

DA – distribution amplifier.
DAT – digital audio tape.
dB – decibel.
DI – direct inject.
Dolby encoding – a pre-emphasis to analogue sound signals before record-ing, to overcome possible losses in quality to high frequencies in the record chain (due to circuit noise, etc.). The sound is decoded upon replay (but not in Beta SP camcorders without playback adaptor).

Dougal – hairy wind sock (named after a character in the children's TV series *Magic Roundabout* (colloq.).

Dub – transfer of information from one medium to another (for example, from one sound track to another, especially in editing).

DV – digital video.

E to E – electronic to electronic.

EDL – edit decision list, a list of shot order for an on-line edit, compiled via an NLE (q.v.) system.

Electret mic – see Section 37, Mics: technical information and operational summaries.

ENG – electronic news gathering.

EQ – equalization, increasing and/or decreasing pre-defined frequency selective bands within sound circuits.

F-run – Free run (timecode option).

FM – Floor Manager *or* frequency modulated, depending on context.

FS – full shot.

Gang – link together two (or more) controls, such that the operation of one is automatically replicated by the others.

Guide track – Soundtrack recorded on location, not intended for broadcast as the main track, thus may be of poor quality, but serves as a useful guide to dialogue, etc. in the scene.

Gun mic – directional mic, may also referred to as shot gun mic.

GV – general view.

Harmonics – combination of frequencies which are multiples of the lowest frequency of the sound source, and which give the distinctive quality/timbre to that source.

HMSF – hours, minutes, seconds and frames (timecode display).

Howl-round – feedback from loudspeaker/s to mics, once above a certain level it becomes self-sustaining, going through the audio chain repeatedly and causing the noise known as 'howl'.

HP – headphones.

HSE – Health and Safety Executive, body responsible for health and safety in the UK.

Hz – hertz (cycles per second).

ID – identification.

Ident. – identify or identification, e.g. with reference to circuits.

Impedance – electrical resistance in a circuit/component, comprising resistance, capacitance and inductance, measured in ohms.

JFMG – Joint Frequency Management Group, body responsible for licensing radio frequencies, for mics and talkback, in the UK.

Lav – lavalier, originally the term referred to a mic worn on a cord around the neck (also known as lanyard), but now may be used in some countries (especially the USA) to indicate a clip mic and/or radio mic.

LI – lithium ion, in this context, a type of rechargeable battery.
LTC – longitudinal timecode.
LU – line-up, a standard check signal using a fixed frequency tone (oscillator generating 1 kHz at 1 mW and fed into 600 ohms, to read 4 on PPM, −4 on VU, −18 or −20 on bar meter: UK).
LS – loudspeaker or long shot, depending on context.

M&E – music and effects, a track carrying precisely that.
M&S – see M/S.
MCU – medium close-up.
Mic – microphone.
Mix/mixed minus – see CF.
MLS – medium long shot.
Moving coil mic – see Section 37, Mics: technical information and operational summaries.
MS – mid shot, or (depending on context):
M/S or **M&S** – middle (or main) and side (NOT mono and stereo) sum and difference signals for stereo reproduction (as opposed to A and B).

Nagra – manufacturer of audio recorders widely used throughout the industry.
NiCad – nickel cadmium, in this context, a type of rechargeable battery.
NICAM – Near Instantaneously Companded Audio Multiplex, the stereo sound encoding system used in many countries for television transmission.
NiMH – nickel metal hydride, another type of rechargeable battery.
NLE – non-linear editing, computer/hard disc editing system enabling ongoing changes to building shot sequences, as opposed to the sequential nature of on-line, tape-based edit systems; often stored as an EDL (q.v.) to transfer to an on-line system.
Noise – amplifiers introduce noise (hiss) into circuits, the greater the amplification, the greater the noise. The signal carried by the circuit needs to be significantly greater than this background noise (specified by the SNR, q.v.).

OMB – one man band (colloq.), similarly OMO – one man operation, see also SPO.
OOF – out of frame.
OOV – out of vision, commentary used with related footage.
OS or **O/S** – over shoulder, often used with 2S, to indicate type of shot, *or* Ordnance Survey, if referring to a map reference, *or* on-site, if referring to a time at a particular location.

PA – public address or Production Assistant, depending on context.
Pad – attenuator, a fixed amount of attenuation to drop the signal level, e.g. 60 dB pad to drop from line level to mic level.
Pan pot – in stereo, control to move mono sound L or R within the sound stage.
PFL – pre-fade listen (also known as pre-hear), monitoring before the fader on a mixer.
Phantom power – condenser mics used in broadcasting are normally capable of being powered via the mic cable. This is known as phantom powering, usually at a level of 48 V.

PO – Post Office, usually a reference to PO jack, or PO lines.
PO jack – Post Office jack, the standard quarter inch (6 mm) headphone connection.
Pot – potentiometer (a variable resistor, e.g. fader).
PPM – peak programme meter.
PR – public relations.
Pre-hear – see PFL.
Presser – press conference (colloq.).
PSC – portable single camera.
PSU – power supply unit.
PTC – piece to camera.

Q&A – Question and answer, a session following a press conference or panel discussion inviting questions from the audience.

R-run – record run (timecode option).
RCD – residual current detector.
R-DAT – DAT recorder with rotating heads.
Recce – reconnoitre.
RF – radio frequency.
Room tone – see wildtrack.
Rushes – film term for the initial (uncorrected) print from the recently developed negative, now taken in television to mean the original recorded pictures and sound (data) on cassette or disc.
R/V – rendezvous, the pre-agreed point to meet on a location, usually stated in conjunction with the call time (using the 24 hour clock).

S-DAT – DAT recorder with stationary heads.
Single – shot framed on one person.
SI unit – Système Internationale unit, the international system of units of measurement (Hz, ohm, etc.)
SNR – signal to noise ratio, measured in decibels.
Sound bite – a single answer, or part thereof, from an interview or vox pop without editing further material from the same piece.
SPO – single person operation.
Sync – synchronous, sound recorded with pictures, but often used to refer to a contributor speaking in vision, as in sound bite.
Syncs – synchronizing pulses, part of the television waveform designed to align the receiver to the transmitted signal to produce stable pictures (and sound).

TB – talkback, part of communications, production information/instructions relayed via separate (lower quality) circuit to main soundtrack.
TBU – telephone balance unit.
TC – Timecode.
Tech reqs – technical requirements, list of technical equipment on the call sheet that production expect the crew to provide.
Tone – see line-up.
T-power – power via mic cable, 9–12 V supply.

Tweaker – screwdriver (colloq.).

VITC – Vertical Interval Timecode (timecode encoded within the vision signal and vertical blanking syncs).
VJ – Video Journalist.
Vox pop – *vox populi* (Latin) literally 'the people's voice', comments within a programme/item from members of the public, normally in vision.
VU – volume units (meter).

Wallpaper – illustrative shots (colloq.).
Wildtrack – recorded separate from pictures, sometimes called 'buzz track', 'atmos.' or 'room tone' (USA).
WS – wide shot.

XLR – external, live and return.

Focal Press

www.focalpress.com
Join Focal Press on-line
As a member you will enjoy the following benefits:

- an email bulletin with **information on new books**

- a regular **Focal Press Newsletter**:

  - featuring a selection of new titles

  - keeps you informed of **special offers, discounts and freebies**

  - alerts you to **Focal Press news and events** such as author signings and seminars

- complete access to **free content** and reference material on the focalpress site, such the focalXtra articles and commentary from our authors

- a **Sneak Preview** of selected titles (sample chapters) *before* they publish

- a chance to have your say on our **discussion boards** and **review books** for other readers

Focal Club Members are invited to give us feedback on our products and services.
Email: worldmarketing@focalpress.com – we want to hear your views!

Membership is **FREE**. To join, visit our website and register. If you require any further informa regarding the on-line club please contact:

> Lucy Lomas-Walker
> Email: l.lomas@elsevier.com
> Tel: +44 (0) 1865 314438
> Fax: +44 (0)1865 314572
> Address: Focal Press, Linacre House,
> Jordan Hill, Oxford, UK, OX2 8DP

Catalogue
For information on all Focal Press titles, our full catalogue is available online at www.focalpres and all titles can be purchased here via secure online ordering, or contact us for a free printed version:

USA
Email: christine.degon@bhusa.com
Tel: +1 781 904 2607 T

Europe and rest of world
Email: j.blackford@elsevier.com
el: +44 (0)1865 314220

Potential authors
If you have an idea for a book, please get in touch:

USA
editors@focalpress.com

Europe and rest of world
focal.press@repp.co.uk